Island in the City

Island in the City

PUERTO RICANS IN NEW YORK

by Dan Wakefield

A CORINTH BOOK
Distributed By The Citadel Press New York
1960

To

*Mary Ann McCoy DeWees, Eileen Fantino Diaz,
and Helen Russell Kahane, who lived and worked
with the children on 100th Street and gave them
not professional advice but what was vital —
food, medicine, and love —*

    this book is dedicated

Acknowledgments

Parts of this book originally appeared in *Harper's Magazine*, *The Nation*, and *Commentary*.

The author would like to thank George Kirstein and *The Nation* for the opportunity to go to Puerto Rico.

Contents

Contents

Into Spanish Harlem

HERMIT MONKS PLAN UNIT IN U.S.;
PLEASED BY "ALONENESS" IN CITY

— A headline in *The New York
Times*, February 17, 1958

THERE IS a moment in the life of New York City, repeated
many times each day, in which the awful separation of our
lives is suddenly crystallized. The track of the New York
Central Railroad rises from underground at 96th and Park and
onto a high, narrow bridge that runs to the north through an
area of tenements and housing projects. Sometimes the passengers glance out the window, and sometimes they catch a fleet-
ing glimpse of a face that stares from a tenement window
beside them. Perhaps for an instant the faces meet; neither one
knows what it sees. The passenger does not know that this is
Spanish Harlem, the oldest of New York City's large Puerto
Rican neighborhoods. The Puerto Rican staring at the train
does not know where it is going, or that it is likely to carry
commuters; indeed, does not know what a commuter is. The
train rumbles on and the faces are left with their own reflec-
tions — the passenger with his in the window of the train, the
Puerto Rican with his in the window of the tenement across
the track. In our mutual blindness we have seen only ourselves.

Our blindness is especially remarkable because there are more than 600,000 Puerto Ricans living in New York City and roughly 200,000 scattered through the rest of the forty-eight states. There are Puerto Ricans living in almost every part of Manhattan, and yet most often they remain in isolation — their settlements soon become crowded ghettos. Spanish Harlem is not the only one of these; it is merely one of the oldest and largest, and in many of its problems the most extreme. The newer ones are being created every day, as older residents react with the fear that greeted so many strangers in the past, crying in dismay that the Puerto Ricans are "taking over" and rushing away to some other spot.

There are, however, in any time a handful of people (we call them "crackpots") who break our society's unwritten laws of isolation. Instead of running from the strangers in fear they go to meet them in friendship. Several years ago, largely by chance, I happened to meet a few such people. In finding them — as perhaps was inevitable — I found East Harlem.

I suppose that my story should begin with Muñoz Marín, but it begins with Mary Ann McCoy. It begins in 1955 when I had an assignment to write about the trial of a group of pacifists who defied the New York State Civil Defense Law, which requires all citizens to participate in the mock atomic air raid drills. These pacifists had gone to the park across from City Hall and quietly sat, in prayer and silent protest, during the scream of the sirens and direction of pedestrians into buildings by the local police. They had given advance notice to the police department of what they intended to do, and a wagon that was waiting by the park picked them up and took them to jail. They were found guilty of violating the law, but sentence was suspended with the judge's admonition that they never do such a crazy thing again. (They have done it again and again, and many of them have now served jail terms for their action.)

I got to know many of the people involved as I covered the story and I learned that many of them were part of a group, or more accurately, part of an idea, known as the Catholic Worker movement, which runs a mission house in the Bowery. Three of the young girls who took part in that first test case on the Civil Defense Law had met one another at the Catholic Worker House and, searching for a way of service for themselves, had opened a kind of day-care center for the children on 100th Street in East Harlem. They also ran a summer camp for the kids, mainly from donations given in response to appeals in the Catholic Worker newspaper. But they found that day care wasn't enough. As daytime residents they were only part of that continual, white, faceless blur of social workers and do-gooders, kindly ladies with large hats and large baskets of charity who occasionally bobbed through the neighborhood and then were gone. They were outsiders, and thus, not trusted. The social workers who come to the neighborhood by day and go home at night often do dedicated work, but it is work that is separated from their own lives, and therefore separated from the lives of the people they work with. The degree of separation of course varies, and some come closer than the lady who has journeyed as a social worker to the neighborhood every day for more than five years and brings with her a sandwich wrapped in wax paper to eat for lunch because she does not consider the local restaurants clean enough to eat in. The three girls from the Catholic Worker did not want their lives to be separated from their work — from the lives of the people they worked with — and they decided that if they worked in East Harlem, and if their work was to have real meaning, they should live in East Harlem.

So it happened that Mary Ann McCoy, Eileen Fantino, and Helen Russell moved into 321 East 100th Street. All of them were white, middle-class, educated, American-born, attractive young girls, and they did not take up this work, as is sometimes the case, because of isolation in their own society.

The building where they moved — as the block itself — is a tenement, and the apartment was in as crumbling a condition as the other apartments around it. The girls fixed it up as best they could, and made it a cheerful place for the children to come. They kept art supplies, toys, and food on hand, and the children — many of whom were not welcome at home — were welcome there. The girls took turns at holding a regular salaried job downtown and one was always at home to keep it open for the kids. The money earned and donations that came from the Catholic Worker all was put in a common fund. When there was any left over it was given to one of the families in need of food. Helen is a nurse, and her professional knowledge increased the help the girls were able to offer.

I went to the girls' apartment for dinner once after the Civil Defense trial was over, and saw East Harlem for the first time. I took the bus going east from 96th and Broadway, through Central Park, across to Third Avenue. I walked north, past the bright, modern lines of the Metropolitan Hospital, up to 100th Street. Third Avenue is bright, lit by the new, glowing bars that replaced the old street lamps with a series of surgical stitches in the black night sky. The Avenues of the neighborhood are, in general, bright — they are where the strangers rush through from north to south, and the path of the passing cars must be illuminated. The streets of the neighborhood are dark — they are only where the people live, and there is little illumination.

One Hundredth Street was dark, filled with life. I turned off Second Avenue into the street, searching for Number 321. I passed the people, and they were dark too, as seemed appropriate for those who lived on this block. For a moment I imagined that if white men lived here very long, they too would turn dark, by laws as irrefutable as the one that would make them dark if they lived on the beach in Florida — except that here the darkness would not be caused by the sun but by the lack of it.

I passed the dark scar of a vacant lot, blistered with refuse, and came to a building that looked like most of the others. The number was 321. I pushed through the door that was patched with raw board where glass once was, and started up the steps. There were voices, in Spanish, and sounds of frying. An odor like dead cats possessed the stairway. On the third floor I knocked at the door of the front apartment, and one of the girls greeted me.

We had roast beef and bread and wine, and talked of the Civil Defense trial and the Catholic Worker and the neighborhood. A knock came at the door and a small boy, his eyes wide, came in carrying a plate at his side. "For my mother," he said. One of the girls took the plate and put a hunk of roast beef on it, and several slices of bread, and the boy backed away, watching the strange feast with wonder.

I left late, and the street was still alive. A group of teen-age boys stood in a doorway, harmonizing on a rock'n'roll song. The rhythm of a tambourine came from down the street at the Pentacostal storefront church's nightly revival. Older men stood outside a barbershop, talking. At the end of the block a policeman twirled his nightstick; whistling, literally, in the dark.

No one who ever sat down at a typewriter could walk through that block without wanting to write about it. I knew I would have to come back, and it was my idea first to do an article of some sort about the neighborhood. But after several trips to it, seeing more, I understood that I was not dealing with just a street or a section of the city, but a "world" — a whole new area of life and death and love and hope and tragedy, moving in a different orbit from the world around it, responding to different pulls and pressures, obeying different laws of action. I was dealing, in other words, not with an article, but with a book. I decided that in order to write such a book I would have to live in that world.

I lived in East Harlem for nearly six months, in tenement rooms on East 100th Street and East 101st Street, and roamed from those places widely through the neighborhood, learning in the limited way that a newcomer can, something of its streets and of its life. But I could not have learned what I did without the help of the Catholic Worker girls and the men and women of the East Harlem Protestant Parish, which has three storefront churches and one of traditional structure in the neighborhood. The Parish was founded in 1949 by a group of young war veterans from New York's Union Theological Seminary, and its ministers and their families live in the same blocks and tenement buildings as the people of the congregation.

The girls and several of the Parish ministers introduced me to friends of theirs, who introduced me to other friends, and their introductions invested me, a stranger, with a borrowed trust that enabled me to talk freely with people, ask them questions, and get their opinions. Perhaps I can give you some hint of how difficult this would otherwise have been by explaining that whenever I happened to be in the neighborhood wearing a suit and tie and was with someone who had not introduced me or identified me, it was often asked first if I were a detective.

Suspicion of strangers, based on bitter experience, is one of the facts of life of this neighborhood. The girls from the Catholic Worker learned it after coming to the same block every day to run their center for the kids and finding they still weren't trusted — and never were until they moved there. The men and women of the East Harlem Protestant Parish who have come to this world to live and work and raise their families are as much a part of the neighborhood as people from another world can possibly become. They are trusted, and yet their presence is often baffling even to the neighbors who know them best. A woman I shall call María Flores, who serves on the Parish Narcotics Committee, told me once about the ministers: "I don't know how these fellows do it. They have college educations, you know; they could do all kinds of things, live in nice houses. I tell you the truth, I don't know why anyone lives here who doesn't have to."

I do not believe that the mystery of why these people live in what has been called one of the world's worst slums can merely be ascribed to religion and stand explained. Many men who claim that their lives are motivated by such a concept live in the most comfortable of circumstances in the most comfortable surroundings. The minister of one of the largest churches in Spanish Harlem is a Puerto Rican who lives in the Bronx. His congregation neither blames him nor thinks it odd. They would be there too, if they had the ticket.

If there is any way to talk about what has brought the
Reverend Norman Eddy from Connecticut to sit up nights
in his home on 100th Street with addicts who are retching and
sweating in the violent pains of withdrawal from heroin; or
what has brought the Reverend George Todd from Gary,
Indiana, to lead the choir of Negro and Puerto Rican members
of his church on 106th Street that he has lovingly trained to
a complex harmony, singing with a joy that has risen above
the neighborhood they live in; if there is any way to explain
these things I do not believe it can be done in sociological
terms. I believe that the closest we can come to understanding
them — to understanding the lives and work of all the men
and women of the Parish — is rather to borrow from the
poetry of Richard Wilbur and say that these people live in
East Harlem because Love has called them to the things of
this world.

This does not mean that these are monklike, long-faced
figures who have given up the good life to move in some as-
cetic realm of sorrowful sacrifice; but rather, as Wilbur means
in his poem, that they have accepted life in its fullest terms.
They are men of good humor as well as good faith, searching
for the real things of this world in a neighborhood where those
things are found in their most extreme form. Perhaps the
worst plague that afflicts the Parish ministers are well-meaning
ladies from the outside world who look at them tearfully and
say, "What wonderful work you have taken up," as if they
were speaking to the volunteers for a one-way rocket trip to
the moon.

There is nothing tearful about Norman Eddy, a tall, vigor-
ous, articulate man in his late thirties, easily spotted walking
down 100th Street by the thick crop of hair that — even be-

fore he moved to this neighborhood — had turned prematurely, totally white. Norm explained to me once that one of the reasons he was so vitally interested in working with narcotics addicts was that the people who were trapped by addiction were forced to come — mentally and physically — face to face with the deepest questions of existence. "Those are the questions I am most interested in," Norm said. And whom could Norman Eddy talk to within, say, the congregation of a comfortable suburban church?

I was sitting in George Todd's apartment one night when the phone rang and it was long distance from Gary, Indiana, with an offer for George to return and become the pastor of his hometown church. George is in his early thirties — though his crew-cut hair and appearance could allow him to pass for a graduate student in an Ivy League college — and the early successful return to the head of his old congregation would be a real honor. He said he would think it over, and after he hung up the phone his wife came into the room and they talked a while about Gary. "You know," George said, "Gary has a lot of problems and a lot of things to be done, but in a way it's easy — you can pick it up and look at it, get a hold of it, see what makes it tick." After a while George said he would write to Gary and thank them for the offer.

Part of the explanation of why these men are here is involved in why Seymour Ostrow, a lawyer who has handled innumerable cases for the members and friends of the Parish, often without a fee, has his practice at 110th and Madison instead of downtown. The desire of Sy Ostrow to practice law in East Harlem and my desire to write a book about it in one way clearly coincides with the desire of the Parish ministers to live and preach there. That is simply the self-rewarding reason that our different work in this neighborhood, whatever else it might be, could never be dull.

But the factors that make the neighborhood a "challenge" for its visitors are the things that make it a tragedy for its natives. George Todd may choose to live in East Harlem all his life, but he will live there always with the knowledge of other offers, other doors. Alicia Robles, who was born on 100th Street, may also live in East Harlem all her life, but if she does it will be because she finds no other doors. These are definitions of a native and a visitor.

One night when I was living on 100th Street I went to visit Mary Ann and her husband on 101st, and Alicia and three of her brothers, who live down the street, happened to be there. Mary Ann and the other Catholic Worker girls had all, in the year before, been married, and were no longer running their center and camp for the kids. But the kids often came around to see Mary Ann, who was still living in the neighborhood.

It was one of the first hot nights of summer, and all hot nights are hotter in East Harlem. The heat accentuates the other unpleasant aspects of life in the slums, as a new color can accentuate the other colors of a painting. The odors and the dirt and the sickness and the crowded conditions are all intensified, deepened, given a new dimension by the heat, and the heat itself is intensified and strengthened in return. There was no breeze, and therefore no "air conditioning." There was no rain, and therefore no cooling spray, like the one that so pleasantly comes from sprinklers set on lawns in summer. There were, of course, no lawns. There was only the street, and its spray was the dust.

It happened that Mary Ann's husband Dan had his brother's car that night, and he came in and suggested that we all go for a ride. The faces of the kids began to beam at the news, and when Dan said we might go to Coney Island, it seemed the kids would grin themselves out of existence. The smallest, Mikey, suddenly ran toward the door and his brother Eddy's hand reached out and caught him by a ragged suspender of the corduroy overalls he wore. He asked Mikey where he was going.

Mikey, who is five, looked up and solemnly announced that he was going home to take a bath. The rest of us laughed, and Mikey's face grew even more serious, until Dan lifted him up and assured him that he didn't have to take a bath to go to Coney Island. Mikey slowly began to beam again.

Alicia began to act as the mother, and herd her brothers together for the trip. Although she was thirteen she looked much younger. Her brown hair hung down long on her neck, and her flimsy green dress was high above her knees and the matchstick legs that were exposed below. When Alicia was twelve she was taken to the hospital and the doctors said that her development as a woman would be retarded because of the malnutrition she suffered from. At thirteen, nearly fourteen, she still had not menstruated. She was, however, the mother of her younger brothers on most occasions. Providencia, the mother of them all (the father had left her), was too busy, too tired, or too sick. Alicia was necessarily a mother before becoming a woman. Neither old enough nor young enough, she played her part and tended her flock. She led them down the stairs, to the car.

We set off out of Harlem to another world — or to many other worlds, for the trip itself was one, the kids already gorging themselves, not on the pizza and ice cream and rides that were to come, but on the new sights and sounds of the drive, and the cool breeze that blew in the windows of the car. They asked about the moon, and the car, and the night, and argued among themselves about the possible answers; the boys switching over to Spanish in the middle of a sentence and Alicia scolding them for it. Whenever they asked her a question in Spanish her answer was, "Please speak English."

All of us were tired and stuffed on the trip back to Harlem, and the kids, except for Alicia, fell asleep. She stayed awake, her face leaning against the half-open window in the back seat, watching the other worlds slip quickly past — the unfamiliar lights and breezes, the shapes and sounds of what was to her, one of its children, a foreign city. The three small boys, in their fitful sleep, began to toss and shift as we neared the neighborhood. It was as if the air itself was enough to stir them to the knowledge of being back. We turned down 101st Street, and Alicia sat up straight and stared out the window. A drunk was weaving a path across the block. Spanish music blared from radios, and men and women sat on chairs and boxes on the sidewalk, fanning themselves and talking. There was no sleep.

"You're home, kids."

Mary Ann pulled up the seat so the kids could get out. Alicia sat without moving for a moment, still staring, and said, not to us or to herself or the people on the street, but rather as if the words had come from inside her and had to be gotten out, like a bitter taste: "I hate this block."

Anyone who doesn't hate the slums — all slums — hasn't been there. Alicia can hate them more than any of us because she was born on 100th Street and because she was raised in its deadly air. She rises up stunted and goes forth in fear, pursuing not "happiness" but survival.

I cannot know the slums or hate them as profoundly as Alicia does because I wasn't born there. I am able to hate them and know them in some small way because of the brief time I lived in Alicia's neighborhood. I cannot approach the abyss of her understanding because no matter what happened I knew I could always escape; I was only a visitor. There were times, though, when I tried with an effort of imagination to extend my experience to that of my neighbors. There were times when I came home tired, late at night, on 100th Street, and climbed the stairs and opened the door of my room and turned the light on and watched the sudden scurry of the cockroaches that moved on the paint-chipped kitchen wall like the scattered filings of a magnet controlled by some invisible force. I would close the door and take a deep breath of the stale, heavy air, and then suddenly I would remember that after all, this wasn't my real home — I would later move on to some clean, well-lighted place like the ones I had lived in before. But then I would close my eyes and concentrate and try to imagine that this was my home and would always be my home and that the clean, well-lighted places of the world were forever closed to me. Most of the time I could not believe it; I could feel nothing. Sometimes, though, for the briefest instant, I could catch a flicker of the nightmare that was only the reality for every other human being beneath that roof. I could feel the enclosure of the flaking walls and see through the window the blackened reflection of the tenement across the street that blocked out the world beyond. But it was only a glimpse.

In the short time that I was a part of this community I sometimes had to take trips outside of it, and in those trips I was often asked about the world I was living in. Once, when I had

lived for several months on 100th Street, the head of a Madison
Avenue business firm told me he wanted to talk to me because
he was very interested in the Puerto Ricans. This was a
happy surprise, and I began to talk about the neighborhood
when the gentleman interrupted me. "What I want to know
is," he said, "what are we going to do about the Puerto
Ricans?" I asked him exactly what he had in mind, and he
said, "I mean isn't there some way we can get them back to
Puerto Rico? They're costing us millions of dollars in tax-
payers' money."

The question was also an answer, in the same way the question of people in the neighborhood who asked if I were a detective was an answer — both are indications of the vast separation of our lives. If the head of that business firm had ever
lived in East Harlem his question would have been, "I wonder
what we are costing the Puerto Ricans?" In my trips outside
the community that is one question I never was asked. It is the
question that was answered for me every day when I lived
there.

Even though I was merely a visitor, there were times when
my own life touched and was touched by the life and death of
the neighborhood. There was the junkie I met at a narcotics
meeting of the Parish who was trying to kick his habit; later
I ran across him on the corner at 100th Street. He was high
again, and he stopped me to talk, hopefully, frantically, of the
possibility of our collaborating on a book about dope — me
doing the writing and him doing the telling. Wasn't there a
lot of money in it? Maybe "They" would buy it as a movie!
We talked about it and he said he would see me at the next
narcotics meeting to talk some more. At the next meeting he
wasn't there, and it was announced that his body, beaten to

death, had been found the night before in the vacant lot on 100th Street.

Because I was involved in some way with the life of the neighborhood I feel a special attachment and responsibility to it, and that is to tell you as meaningfully as possible what it is like. I am not a sociologist or anthropologist, and I do not have the intentions of those professions to analyze or theorize. I am a reporter and I have the intention of a reporter — to tell you what it is like. If I were a poet, I might be able to do a better job. I do not say that lightly, for I believe that of all that has ever been written about Harlem, no one has said half so much as García Lorca, the Spanish poet who came to New York for a year and wrote several poems about Harlem that capture its essence more purely than anything I have ever read. But, unfortunately, I am not a poet and I will have to do my best as a reporter.

Most of this book is concerned with things I have seen and heard. I describe them to you. I tell you about them, and sometimes about their history. I do not claim that in doing this I am telling you all there is to tell, or that I possibly could know all there is to know about a world as rich and as deep as the world of Spanish Harlem. The frustration of trying to convey an essence of something this large and this human was expressed much better than I could say it by a boy from the neighborhood. The boy (if we can call someone who has known the hell of heroin addiction a boy) was present one night when a reporter from a New York newspaper was in the neighborhood to get some information on how the Narcotics Committee of the East Harlem Protestant Parish tried to help the local addicts. Several addicts were present, including this boy, who had been to the narcotics hospitals at Riverside and Lexington and said that the only place he felt he got any real help was from the people of the Parish. He explained that their doors were always open at any time of the day or night, and that their faith in him and his possible recovery never flagged no matter how many times he fell back into the habit. The reporter said yes, all that was fine, but couldn't he give some statistics, something *specific?* The boy thought for a moment and said very quietly, "You know, there are some things just too heavy to put on paper."

Some of the things I would like to convey are just too heavy to put on paper. I cannot tell you everything — but I can tell you more than you know. If you want to know everything you will have to wait until the time — unknown, unpredictable, but all the same, inevitable — when a young Puerto Rican who was born in East Harlem writes a first novel. Then you will really know all about it, and not until then.

I have referred, and will refer, to the world I am talking about as both Spanish Harlem and East Harlem. I use the two names interchangeably, although there is a certain distinction. The Puerto Rican settlement in the section of New York City known as East Harlem, which covers the northeastern tip of Manhattan island, grew up after the First World War. At first it was mainly concentrated between Fifth and Lexington Avenues, from about 100th to 120th Streets, and was known as *El Barrio* ("The District" or "The Neighborhood") and also as Spanish Harlem. During that early period, in the 1920's and 1930's, there existed beyond it in the rest of East Harlem the largest Italian and the largest Russian Jewish communities in the city. But the Spanish part of the area has steadily grown and the Italian, Jewish, and an already dwindling Irish settlement have steadily diminished. The Spanish section, which

once was a part of the world of East Harlem, has come to en-
compass nearly all that world. There are no strict lines that
seal off the Puerto Rican residents, but their southern boundary is generally regarded as 96th Street. As Pee-Wee, who
hails from 100th Street, explains it, "You go below 96th
Street, you're going South of the Border." To the north, from
116th Street on, the Spanish section merges with Negro districts in the west and gives way to the last of the old Italian
colony on the east. All of the neighborhood east of Third
Avenue was once mainly an Italian section, with scattered
Puerto Rican blocks, but that proportion has been largely reversed, with the addition of many Negro residents since World
War II. The last of the Italian stronghold has shrunk to the
area around 116th to 125th Street, from Third Avenue to the
East River. Negroes live throughout all of East Harlem, but
Fifth Avenue serves as a fairly firm western boundary be-
tween Spanish Harlem and the main Negro section of Central
Harlem, which has few Puerto Ricans.

Most strictly speaking then, Spanish Harlem today means
most of East Harlem except for the upper or northern section.
The newspaper *El Diario*, which has the largest circulation of
any Spanish language newspaper in the city, refers in its col-
umns to "East Harlem," *El Barrio*, and Spanish Harlem (*El
Harlem Hispano*) interchangeably — and so will I.

Just as this story is not a clear-cut, easy composition in black
and white, neither are its geographic boundaries; there is a
point at which geography becomes meaningless or even misleading. I believe there is hardly a block in all of Spanish Harlem that does not have at least several families left from the
older settlements of Jews, Irish, or Italians — those who were
left behind when the others moved up to neighborhoods of

higher economic condition. I remember waking one morning on East 101st Street to hear a deep, echoing voice singing in a thick Irish brogue. I went to the window, and down six floors below in the cement square that was hemmed in on every side by the tenements — the place where the garbage cans are kept — a white-haired, partly crippled man held out a battered hat and sang "My Wild Irish Rose" while the Puerto Rican women came to the windows and flung down coins that he hobbled to collect.

There are beautiful things that happen here and also terrible things. I have left nothing out of this book because it would reflect badly on this or that party or group. I have in some instances substituted names when use of a person's real name could be harmful to him. Most of the names, however, are the names of the real people. Since there are terrible things that happen here, and since this is a book about a Puerto Rican community, I suppose there are those who will say that this reflects badly on the Puerto Ricans. I would remind them that this is also a book about the slums, and I would ask such people to consider what causes these things to happen — a life of poverty and ill health in one of the world's worst slums, or the fact of being a Puerto Rican.

It is part of this sad chronicle that we see, or should see, that the problems that come up in it are not so much "Puerto Rican Problems" as problems that the Puerto Ricans have inherited from the rest of us. They are part of what we are costing the Puerto Ricans.

I hope you will also realize, through the people you meet and the things you see in the pages that follow, that the Puerto Ricans are individual people — some good, some bad, some fat, some thin. The Puerto Ricans are José Ferrer, a movie star, and José Morales, a textile worker; they are Frank Santana, who is serving a prison term, and Rusty Morales, who is studying for a graduate degree in social work; María Flores, a secretary, and Joe Roman, a newspaperman; Ricardo Sánchez, a migrant from the sugar fields, and Tony Mendez, a Tammany Hall politician.

But now I am going to stop my talking and let the people and the scenes and the faces talk. "I" have introduced you and now I will no longer be in the book. I am not a part of what happens, and I would only clutter it up. What I have seen and what I am going to tell you is too dramatic to be made any more so by my sticking my head in and saying, "Look, isn't this something?" I have told you what I think in this introduction and now it is up to you to think.

May you think well, and may you become involved in this life. May its faces haunt you and its dialogues disturb you. May its tragedies sicken you and its love make you glad, and may you, if only in your mind, if only for a moment, become a part of Spanish Harlem.

Island in the City

Long Night's Journey

It is no good to be poor.

— RICARDO SÁNCHEZ, a
Puerto Rican migrant

RICARDO SÁNCHEZ came from where the sugar cane is higher than a man to the plaza in old San Juan where the buses marked *Aeropuerto* stop. He came with his wife and two daughters and three suitcases and a paper bag and the promise from a brother in Harlem, New York, that there was work to be found in *fábrica*. The work in the sugar cane was over for the season and Ricardo had found nothing else. The government would pay him $7 every two weeks for thirteen weeks before the season began again, and then with the season he would get $3.60 a day for eight hours in the sun. He had done it before, as his fathers had done it, but this time he told himself he wanted something more. "It is," he said, "no good to be poor." His lean brown face was twisted in a grimace of disgust as he said the words, and remained that way, in the memory of poverty, slowly relaxing as he fingered the three fountain pens neatly clipped to the pocket of his new brown suit, and turned to face the dark from where the buses come.

Christopher Columbus, migrant by trade, stood by frozen in the stone of a statue, the accidental patron saint of the plaza that serves as a boarding place for those who go away. Even more practically, Columbus' weathered figure serves those who stay, for around it sit the old men who sit around the statues of the plazas of the world; these by the chance of Columbus' mistaken discoveries (and Ponce de León's mistaken hopes) speaking the language of his creditor the Queen. But the Queen is four centuries dead, and the island's highest ruler is a president from Kansas — a place whose name and language are totally foreign to the old men who sit by the statue.

Their fathers before them were Indians here, called Borinqueños, and Spanish followers of Ponce de León, seeker after gold and youth and captor of neither. His body is buried up the street. Their fathers were Negro slaves from Africa, brought here to fill the vacuum left when the Indians painfully vanished, by death and escape, from the Spaniards' rule. The Spaniards built great forts and repulsed the futile attacks of the French and the Dutch and Sir Francis Drake and ruled until 1898. It was then, a year after Spain had finally granted the people of the island a form of self-government, that Admiral Sampson bombarded San Juan and General Nelson Miles led his troops to the island soil with the news that he had brought "the advantages and blessings of enlightened civilization from the United States of America" and the island again was a colony without self-rule. The old Spanish walls of the city were broken at last, and to the east of the plaza of Christopher Columbus there stands today a building of the YMCA where there once stood one of the four city gates. The only gate remaining is used now not to keep enemies out but to draw tourists in. Across from the *Alcaldia* — the City Hall — constructed by the Spanish in 1604, is the New York Department Store, proclaiming in Spanish a sale in which "Everything Goes." Below the iron grillwork balconies of the Old San

Juan Bar and Grill a sign in the window reads "Real Italian Pizza." A taxicab crawls through the narrow stone streets like an insect caught in a maze, turning the high-walled corners with painstaking care. The city is quiet, and the old men who sit in the plaza seem unconcerned. Their fathers are gone and their sons are free to go.

For more than a century the sons have left the plazas and the dust-and-green towns of the interior to come to New York. Ricardo Sánchez is young, but his journey is old. The first Puerto Ricans came to New York in the early 1800's, along with other men of good hope from the underfed islands of the Caribbean who decided that "it is no good to be poor." From Cuba and Santo Domingo they came, from San Juan and Haiti and Jamaica. Some survived and others were lost, and in 1838 the men from Puerto Rico who had managed to make themselves merchants of New York City formed a Spanish Benevolent Society for those of their brothers who had failed and were hungry.

Others went west, and by 1910 there were Puerto Ricans living in thirty-nine states of the Union. Twenty years later the people of the island were in every state, though the great majority were still in New York City. The journey north from the Caribbean became a regular route for those seeking something better (and having the money to make the search), and for most of the first half of the twentieth century an average of 4000 came from Puerto Rico to the mainland every year.

No one seemed to notice. It was not until near the end of the Second World War that the quiet, steady migration became the great migration — the promise of the mainland suddenly expanding with more new jobs than ever before and the word passing on from relative to relative, friend to friend, employment recruiter to unemployed. During the war there was little transportation available for Puerto Ricans who wanted to leave the island, but toward the end of it the U.S. War Manpower Commission brought workers up in army transports to help fill the booming job market. In the first year after the war 39,900 Puerto Ricans came to the mainland, and the annual stream reached an average of roughly 50,000 in the postwar decade. As it has throughout its history, the Puerto Rican migration curve followed the business curve on the mainland, and the start of the greatest postwar recession in 1957 was reflected by a 28 per cent decrease in migration from the year before. Downturns in the volume of business on the continent have always meant downturns in migration from the island, and during the worst depression years of the thirties the flow of migrants actually reversed itself, with more returning annually to the island than came from it. But barring an extreme and prolonged depression, the total of 600,000 first- or second-generation Puerto Ricans in New York City in 1958 was expected to rise to a million by the early 1970's. And, for the first time, the great migration had begun to spread more heavily in cities and towns throughout the country. In 1950, 85 per cent of the entering migrants settled in New York City, but by 1956 and 1957 the average was down to 65 per cent, with others going to expanding Puerto Rican settlements in cities such as Philadelphia (New York's largest Spanish-language newspaper now carries a special column of Puerto Rican news from Philadelphia), Chicago, Cleveland, Ashtabula, Bridgeport, Milwaukee, and others farther west.

The journey from the island had become not only more promising because of the market for jobs after World War II but also much easier to make because of the airplanes that rose from San Juan and landed at Idlewild, New York City, 1600 miles up the ocean, in only eight hours and for only $75 on regular airlines instead of the former price of $180. Besides the approved commercial lines that opened up regular service after the war there were secondhand planes making unscheduled flights for $35 — they could charge that price because they were paid off later by men from the states who came to Puerto Rico and charged "employment agent" fees that often consumed life savings sweated from sugar cane as payment for nonexistent jobs in New York City. Some of the victims never found out because they first became the victims of ill-equipped planes that crashed in the ocean. After several such tragedies the government outlawed the small, unscheduled airlines from making the San Juan–New York run.

But the regular, legal air travel flourished — not only giving a boost to the old migration to the mainland cities but also opening up a new migration. Cheap and fast plane travel made it possible to transport idle agricultural workers from Puerto Rico during the heavy harvesting season on the mainland in the spring, and back again to the island when the sugar-cane season began in the fall. A new seasonal migration began on that basis after the war and has grown to an annual flow of about 30,000 workers (not counted in the regular migration figures of those who come and plan to stay). Contrary to popular belief, the great majority of Puerto Ricans who come to New York, and other U.S. cities, are not laborers but city people who have held city jobs on the island.

Ricardo Sánchez, who waited in the dark for the bus marked *Aeropuerto*, was one of the small but slowly growing number of Puerto Ricans who have left the sugar-cane fields for the city. The desire to escape from the backbreaking work of the cane cutting is still not easily fulfilled, but the dream has become much more widespread since many young men saw the world in service with the U.S. Army in Korea, and returned home with higher aspirations. Frank Ruiz, the secretary-treasurer of the *Sindicato Azucarero* (Sugar Workers Union) in Puerto Rico says that it is harder now to get the young men to work in the cane fields because "the army has refined them."

Ricardo Sánchez was able to make at least a partial transition in his work before the drastic change from the island fields to the New York fabric shops. During the idle season a year before, he had found a job doing piecework in a garment shop in the small town of Vega Baja. But the work didn't last, and after another season in the fields he decided to try his luck — and his brother's help — in the *fábrica* shops of New York City.

Ricardo held for himself and his family tickets on the $52.50 night coach Thrift Flight to Idlewild airport. It leaves six nights a week from San Juan at eleven o'clock and arrives the next morning at Idlewild at seven. The adjective "thrift" is the only term of distinction between this flight and the other night coach flight, which costs $64, leaves a half hour later, and arrives in New York City two hours earlier. The Thrift Flight is not recommended — or even suggested at the ticket counters — to non-Puerto Rican travelers. English-speaking people who ask about it are told that it is better to spend the extra money and go on the eleven-thirty flight.

There were only Puerto Ricans on the *Aeropuerto* bus that Ricardo Sánchez boarded in the plaza of Christopher Columbus. They stayed together when they reached the San Juan airport, checking in baggage and then joining friends and relatives and watchers in the crowd on the observation deck. When the flight was called, it was as if a troop plane were leaving for a war, or a group of refugees being shipped of necessity out of their native country. It is that way every night around eleven o'clock at the San Juan airport — the women crying and the men embracing them; the old people staring out of wrinkled, unperceiving faces and the young engrossed with the wonder, rather than the pain of it, pressing up against the iron rail of the observation deck and squinting through the dark to watch the line of human travelers move as if drawn by a spell through the gate below and into the still, silver plane that swallows them, closing silver on silver to complete itself, and then slowly moves toward the dark and disappears.

Inside the airplane Ricardo Sánchez had seated his wife and one of his daughters on the left-hand, two-seat aisle, and taken his other daughter and himself across to the right in the three-seat row with a stranger. The flight was full, as these flights are nearly always full. The $52.50 night flights run by both Eastern and Pan American airlines from San Juan to New York are booked for days in advance.

The plane was hot — hotter than the 75° weather outside — and many of the men, already sweating, had taken off their coats. A young, dark-skinned woman in an aqua silk dress was crying softly and fanning herself with the plastic *Occupado* sign from the pocket of the seat in front of her. The stewardess appeared at the head of the aisle when the door was closed and gave a demonstration while the steward explained on the loudspeaker, first in Spanish and then in English, the instructions for putting on life jackets in case of an emergency.

The engines began, swelled, and the plane crept forward. The woman in the aqua dress pressed her face against the porthole-style window, crying much louder now. The balcony of watchers grew smaller and darker; became a few white handkerchiefs waved in the night, and then was gone. Babies began to cry as the plane rose, moving above the red, white, and green pinpoints strung geometrically and sparkling in the pattern of the city and suburbs of San Juan. In several minutes the dark had covered it. The no-smoking and safety-belt signs in the plane blinked off, the overhead lights went out, and only the small, individual reading lights above the seats were on. The babies stopped crying, and the temperature of the plane began to cool. Seats were pushed back, and soon the thin beams of light from the few remaining reading lights were thickened with cigarette smoke. The stewardess came by and asked Ricardo Sánchez if he wanted her to hang up his suit coat. The stewardess did not speak Spanish and Ricardo, looking at her quizzically and smiling politely, clutched his coat when she reached for it and held it folded on his lap. He leaned his head back against the seat, folding his hands on his lap, and stared straight ahead, the view slightly tilted with the angle of the seat; his mouth in a tight, tentative smile. After a while he closed his eyes.

The dull, steady roar of the engine was the single sound, growing louder and fuller as other sounds stopped, until, in its constant drone and throb, the sound of the engine became no sound at all, but a part of the plane's suspended life. It became a sound again several hours later when the screams woke Ricardo Sánchez from his tilted sleep:

"Ay, ay, *ayyyy!*"

The women screamed as the plane fell forward through the dark. The sound of the two engines heightened and throbbed. The plane leveled off from the drop, leaving the stomachs of the passengers with the sickening, overturned sensation that comes on a roller coaster during the sudden, steep descent. The steward hurried down the aisle with smelling salts.

Ricardo Sánchez leaned forward to look across the aisle at his wife. Her head was leaning across on her daughter, who sat in silence, her eyes widening to watch the steward stop by the seat and wave the smelling salts. Ricardo's mouth opened and his white teeth were clenched together as if he were being struck. He started up, but the safety belt was fastened on his waist. He looked at it a moment, then leaned back into his seat. The plane dipped again.

The steward stopped and explained to the only non-Puerto Rican passenger that the plane had hit a storm.

"We felt it quite a bit," he said. "The planes for this flight aren't pressurized. If you take the eleven-thirty flight — the $64 one — you fly above all this."

There was no announcement in Spanish about the storm. Ricardo Sánchez's wife, revived, pulled the white bag for vomiting out of the pocket of the seat and leaned into it. Lightning flashed as the plane pitched again in the dark — the tiny green light on the end of the wing was the only thing visible. Ricardo Sánchez tightened the safety belt of his daughter who sat next to him. She clutched at the arm of the seat, in silence, and pressed against the back of it, her thin legs sticking out with the shiny black patent leather shoes not touching the floor. Her father stroked her hair, then leaned back himself and touched the palms of his hands together, pointing upward, in his lap. Through the crack of the seat in front, the brown, large-veined hands of a woman twisted and knotted and pulled on a rainbow-colored silk handkerchief.

The dips became slighter and the screams lower, several

becoming soft, continual moans that rose with the fall of the plane. A man walked back to the stewardess who sat reading a copy of the *Saturday Evening Post* and asked her in English if the worst of the storm was over. She looked up annoyed and said, "*I'm* not the pilot," touched her forefinger to her tongue, and flipped the page of the magazine.

A little after five o'clock in the morning the silver wings of the plane became visible, and then a layer of clouds below the plane. A pink strip grew at the end of the layer of clouds in the east, and an orange streak grew from the pink. The billowed layers of clouds below became blue-gray, then lighter blue. Ricardo Sánchez tapped his daughter's shoulder and told her to look. She leaned across on his lap and he explained, "It is dawn. Look — it is beautiful."

About six o'clock the stewardess came by with a tray of steaming paper cups and asked each passenger, in English, "Would you like some coffee?" Some didn't seem to understand so the stewardess repeated the question in more distinct tones, "Would you like some coffee?" There were those who still did not understand and the stewardess, seemingly annoyed, passed on. Some people nodded, or held out their hands, and were given coffee.

The woman in the aqua silk dress stood up in the aisle and pulled up her stockings. She sat back down, pulled a small bottle from her purse, turned it on her finger, and dabbed at her neck. The strong, sweet smell of perfume spread across the aisle. The plane had broken through the clouds and there was water below. Soon there was land — another island; this one, too, striped and set with rows of white lights and green lights, fewer lights in the growing gray dawn than were seen in the night above San Juan. The island that the plane approached seemed not so much larger than the island it had left. Lower, the land turned brown and barren, with a swamplike series of protrusions in the water, and the plane moved closer till the brown high grass on the land and the wind-ruffled waves of the water were clearly visible. The plane seemed about to touch the water and suddenly touched on land — the end of the Idlewild airstrip. The babies again were crying.

The plane stopped, and the passengers looked out the window at the quiet runways, the long, low buildings, and the high, silver lampposts that arched in a long and graceful curve like the neck of some thin and watchful animal, repeated row on row. The women stepped out of the silver door, clutching at their flimsy, bright-colored dresses, into the morning chill of New York and the gray, surrealistic landscape of Idlewild.

Friends and relatives waited at the gate with scarves and coats and kisses and handclasps and took the passengers out of the airport and into cars and buses to the Bronx and the lower East Side and the upper West Side of Manhattan and also to New York's first large Puerto Rican neighborhood, known as Spanish Harlem.

The landscape of Harlem is dark and loud. The sky and the land do not lie in sheets of pale, unbroken color as they do at Idlewild airport. There is no room. Sky and land are everywhere blocked and blemished by stone — old, smoke-and-weather-stained tenements grafted together in grassless blocks; raw, new walls of housing projects rising in brown, identical forms that stand together in arbitrary clusters like squads of dumb and paralyzed giants stuck in the mud they grow from. At 96th Street the long, fenced-in plots of lawn that run through the center of Park Avenue disappear, and in their place the New York Central Railroad rises from underground onto an elevated track that stretches north on Park, making a straight, black spine through Spanish Harlem. In its shadow to the west from 109th and 116th Streets is *La Marqueta* — the open market place of fruits and fish and shirts and shoes and dresses and vegetables, owned mainly by Italians and Jews, sold mainly to Puerto Ricans. Goods are displayed on tables outside the store, some in the open, some underneath the awnings like the one that reads "Harry Schwartz Infants' and Children's Wear — *Se habla español.*" Growing out of the shadows of the soot-covered railroad bridge, west to Fifth Avenue, east to the East River, is the world of Spanish Harlem.

In winter the children build bonfires in vacant lots, and the tropics is only a memory, preserved by signs and language. The past on the island and the promise of New York are intermingled, and flow out of separate identities into a single experience, a single mixture, that is neither one thing nor the other. In old San Juan was the New York Department Store; in Harlem, New York, is the San Juan Restaurant. The wall of a coffee shop in old San Juan bore a sign advertising the flight to New York; the sign in a barbershop on Lexington Avenue advertises *La Isla Encantada*. "The Enchanted Island" was supposed to be New York, but it turns out to be Puerto Rico.

"Enchanting" becomes an adjective of mockery when used to describe the slums of Harlem, and yet that is only a recent reality. Harlem was once known as "Happy Valley" and described as an area of "brownstone fronts and Saratoga trunks." Carl H. Pierce reported in a history of Harlem that during the eighteenth century "prosperous New Yorkers turned to the beautiful rolling land at the upper end of the island in search of summer homes, and newcomers from over the sea found within its borders scenic charms and conditions of life greatly to be desired." The word "Harlem" has come to mean Negro and slum to the world at large; it once meant Dutch and suburban, and later on, Irish and Jewish and middle class. But despite these changes the history of Harlem contains a curious continuity. It has always, for someone, meant Utopia. It has always, for someone, signified the end of a journey.

Its founders were migrants from Holland, religious refugees who landed in 1658 in that moment later imagined by Scott Fitzgerald in *The Great Gatsby* when he "became aware of the old island here that flowered once for Dutch sailors' eyes — a fresh, green breast of the new world." The Dutch sailors landed at the northern tip of Manhattan and named it New Haarlem. The heritage was fitting, for the old town of Haarlem had once become famous as a city of migrants when its men followed Frederick Barbarossa on the great crusade to Jerusalem. New Haarlem became the new Jerusalem, first for the refugees from Europe and next for the eighteenth-century dwellers of downtown Manhattan who had enough money to move to the rich Happy Valley of Harlem.

Poverty first disturbed the Happy Valley in the nineteenth century, when Irish squatters settled in what is now the northern tip of Central Park. The Irish immigrants built small shacks and kept goats in the yard, and the area they occupied soon became known as Goatville among the old established citizens. In the 1890's Harlem was invaded again — this time by the elevated tracks, and the land's remote, suburban character was lost in the new connection with the rest of New York.

It was not until after the Irish and the El that the Negroes came. The first of them came in the early 1900's, and more

who wanted to migrate from midtown were halted by landlords' restrictions until a sudden, unexpected break was made.
The Pennsylvania Railroad selected the site for its terminal
in a section that was then largely occupied by Negroes, and
bought for resettlement of tenants a row of large houses at
135th and Lenox, in central Harlem. The Negroes moved in
and whites from surrounding neighborhoods moved out. More
Negroes came into the gap, and by 1910 the name of Harlem
had begun to be recognized as the name of a Negro community.

But from Fifth Avenue to the East River — East Harlem —
there were still no Negro residents, and the population was
principally of Russian Jewish, Italian, and Irish origin. It was
into the lower part of that section that the Puerto Ricans first
began to move after World War I, and thus eventually give
the name of Harlem another new dimension and descriptive
adjective — this time, "Spanish." There were other Spanish-
speaking people there too, from Cuba, the Dominican Republic, and a very few from Spain itself. But the adjective that
translates into "Spanish" to describe this new world of Harlem
does not mean "from Spain," which would make the name of
the neighborhood *El Harlem Español*. It is called, rather, *El
Harlem Hispano*, meaning "Hispanic" or "of Spanish tradition
and origin" in the broadest sense of language and culture.
Outsiders might have imagined that the new community ought
to be called *El Harlem Portorriqueño* or *El Harlem Borin-
queño*, meaning Puerto Rican Harlem, since the great majority
of its residents were Puerto Ricans. But the migrants from the
island very seldom refer to themselves as Puerto Ricans. The
name of the newest and poorest class of New Yorkers has become a stigma that few want to bear, and they go to great

lengths to avoid it. Some, especially business and professional men who have moved away from the poorer neighborhoods and often sought to remove themselves completely from their brothers, have been known to tell outsiders they are Dominicans, Cubans, or South Americans. "It's easier," one man from Puerto Rico who calls himself a Dominican said. "You don't have to explain anything." Those who do not go so far as to claim another home still don't specifically claim their own home. They call themselves *Hispano* or, to the English-speaking outsider, "Spanish."

Before the local migration that created Spanish Harlem, the Puerto Ricans had existed literally on the fringe of New York. Their two small settlements were located close to where they got off the boat from the island, and they huddled there, balancing on the outer rim of the life of the city, never presuming to penetrate farther. The first of the colonies was begun by a group of cigarmakers who stopped at the entry point and place of first settlement of so many streams of immigrants, the lower East Side. The other was the Navy Yard section of Brooklyn, where a group of Puerto Rican seamen settled within sight of the docks they departed from.

The sea route provided the only means of entry from Puerto Rico in those days, and the sea route was largely responsible for the original choice of New York as the place for Puerto Ricans to settle in the United States. New York was the destination of the great majority of Puerto Ricans who wanted to come to the mainland. The only other regular continental stops that were made by ships from San Juan were the Gulf Coast ports, and they were less frequently run and more expensive than the $40, three- to five-day voyages to New York City. It has sometimes been questioned why the Puerto Rican migrants, who have to adjust to a new, cold climate in New York City, didn't take the Gulf coast route and settle in the South, where living and working conditions were more familiar. Aside from the obstacles of money and accessibility, the Puerto Ricans had to face the question of color. The Spanish-Negro-Indian heritage of the island has produced a variety of skin color, ranging from Negro to white with all shades in between, and an estimated one-fourth of the Puerto Ricans are of Negro complexion. The point of migration was — and is — to find a better life, and the South was obviously not the answer for workers of dark complexion.

New York was at least a workable answer, though not without its problems for people of color. But the darker-skinned migrants did not face the new discrimination of the mainland with all the innocence that often is believed. Because there is no legal discrimination based on color in Puerto Rico, it is commonly simply stated that "there is no discrimination." But the darker-skinned people on the island are seldom found in office or professional positions, or in the top hotels, night clubs, or social activities. When the Puerto Ricans meet discrimination on the mainland, it is not altogether a new experience.

María Flores, who came to East Harlem from the island as a child, had her own native information to contribute when a Negro friend of hers began to talk one night about discrimination in the States. Lucy Dale, a Negro woman who came to East Harlem from Massachusetts, lives with her three children in a typically crowded and crumbling two-room apartment on East 105th Street. María had stopped by to visit one evening, and Lucy began to talk about the bill to eliminate discrimination in New York housing that was then being hotly debated in the City Council. The two women sat drinking coffee in the "living" room of the brown-walled, scarred interior that is the same interior of thousands of other old-law tenement rooms in the neighborhood, and they talked of the law that would mean at least a theoretical escape from these surroundings. Lucy knew of a Negro musician who hadn't been able to get an apartment closer to his work in midtown Manhattan, and she said what a shame it was that "even in New York" it was like that.

María, whose smooth tan skin is lighter than the brown complexion of Lucy, agreed that there was plenty to complain of here, but said there were also things to be glad about — like jobs. Both women work in East Harlem as secretaries, and María said, "If I was back in San Juan, I wouldn't have any office job. You don't see girls my color in an office — unless they're cleaning up or something. Or maybe if they know some judge or politician. I suppose if I went back and really tried and got some pull I might be able to make it, but I'd still be lucky."

Lucy said she'd never been to Puerto Rico and didn't know what it was like, but she'd always wanted to go for a visit — maybe take a vacation there someday. She wondered if she'd run into trouble like "that." She laughed and said, "I don't have to go all the way down there to have that kind of trouble."

"No," said María, "you won't unless you try to stay at one of the big hotels on the beach — you'd have trouble there, in the swanky places. But remember if you go you shouldn't take a lot of sport clothes or shorts — just dresses. It's all right for those little American girls to go down there and parade around the streets in shorts, but you might get taken for one of us, and the Puerto Rican women just can't do that."

María was dressed at the moment in a sweater, black toreador pants, and sneakers, and wore horn-rimmed glasses that slid back into her curly black hair. She shook her head back and forth with the emphasis of an independent woman who is proud of her independence and said, "That's another reason I'd never go back there to live. I'm used to living my own life."

María has had to live her own life — make her own life — by herself, for her husband left her with three small children to support. She has done it without any help from the state or the family, and in doing it moved much farther in spirit, if not in distance, from the world of her parents. They live in East Harlem too, just a few blocks away from María, but they speak only Spanish and do not altogether approve of María's friends who speak only English, or — like María — speak both Spanish and English and often choose to speak English. But María has always been something of a family outsider — she was born that way. This, she says, is what it is like:

"I'm the darkest one in my family. I was always being 'explained away.' I don't mind that any more, but what I can't take is the way my parents won't face the facts. They never would really admit my color, even to me. My mother told me we were Puerto Ricans, and Puerto Ricans were white. I remember I came home from school one day and I told my mother a boy in my class was as black as my shoes, and he spoke Spanish. She told me no, if that boy spoke Spanish, he was white."

The darkest-skinned member of a Puerto Rican family often complains that he is the "lowest" in the family, and has to do all the work around home and gets little reward. The Reverend Norman Eddy, who has worked for more than five years with narcotics addicts in the neighborhood, has observed that in almost every case the Puerto Rican addict is the darkest-skinned member of his family. "He may actually have very light skin, but if you meet his family you almost always see that his skin is darker than the others in the family."

Life on the mainland has, if anything, heightened the Puerto Ricans' color consciousness, for they are anxious not to be identified as American Negroes. It doesn't take long to learn that the Negroes are lowest on the scale in American life, and in order not to be like them the darker Puerto Ricans are often the most reluctant to learn English. Speaking only Spanish identifies them as foreign and therefore not just a Negro. The Puerto Ricans in New York City have learned the consciousness of color from both their old home and their new home, and that accumulated knowledge has brought them to the awful moments of fear and hope when the pregnant women in Spanish Harlem rub their stomachs with talcum powder to make the baby turn out light.

Like a shadow of their own dark fear, the Puerto Ricans are followed by American Negroes. The Negroes followed them into East Harlem, which had been a white neighborhood, and later into other places where the Puerto Ricans broke the color barrier in housing and automatically enabled Negroes to cross the line afterwards. The Jews of the neighborhood said that East Harlem was no longer desirable because the Puerto Ricans were moving in. Later on many Puerto Ricans said the neighborhood was no longer desirable because the Negroes were moving in. But the Puerto Ricans were not as easily able to move somewhere else. Those who were able moved to the Puerto Rican settlement in the Morrisania section of the

Bronx; and the Puerto Rican community in East Harlem soon became known as a home for the poor. By 1927 the Puerto Rican Brotherhood of New York City was publishing an appeal for their brothers not to discredit the Puerto Ricans who lived in East Harlem. The Brotherhood sadly observed that many times Puerto Ricans in the city discredited *El Barrio* and that some of the most hateful remarks and rumors about that neighborhood came from other Puerto Ricans "who live on salaries in offices who think themselves superior."

The Bronx became known as *El Barrio de los adaptos;* Harlem was the home of the unadapted. But Harlem was hard to escape, not only because of financial reasons, but also because of housing discrimination in other areas. In the thirties the New York Spanish newspaper *La Prensa* printed a cartoon that embodied this frustration. One half of the cartoon pictured a fat, cigar-smoking American in a Spanish country, saying that he had *muchos pesos* and wanted to find a place to live. Two small Spaniards bowed before him, and bade him welcome to a fine house. The other side of the cartoon, marked "Washington Heights," showed an American woman waving a broom at a prospective tenant and saying "Get out! No Spanish people are allowed here."

Since that time many Puerto Ricans managed to penetrate the white lines of Washington Heights, and sections all over the city that were formerly barred to them. In 1958 there were Puerto Ricans living in all the health districts (the smallest city district breakdown) of New York, and heavy settlements on the upper West Side, the lower East Side, and the Bronx. But there still was East Harlem — more crowded than ever, more "Spanish" than ever, and still just as poor. The older groups who once were newcomers mostly had managed to move up the ladder, out of this slum. Italian groceries became *Bodegas.* Synagogues became Pentecostal churches with signs of services printed in Spanish.

On East 100th Street a storefront synagogue had to be sold to a Negro–Puerto Rican church because the old congregation was no longer large enough. The sale was in the summer, and the few remaining families of the synagogue asked the new owners if they might hold services on the sidewalk in front on Sabbath evenings. The request was granted, and the dozen or so members of the departed synagogue gathered on Fridays at dusk on folding chairs on 100th Street in front of their former temple. The weather grew colder and the crowd grew smaller on each succeeding Friday and then the first snow came, and after that the services were no longer held. When the good weather came again there were no more requests for the sidewalk synagogue meeting. The synagogue had died on the street, which is finally appropriate in Spanish Harlem, where so much has its birth and death on the street and the street holds so much life; and is, at times, alive itself.

When the good weather comes the chairs and tables come out to the sidewalk for checkers games and dominoes and sometimes cards, and the kids come out, the young ones playing in the vacant lots, the older ones huddled by candy stores and late at night in hallways of tenements, harmonizing. But the street comes most alive in the late afternoon when the men return home from work and the kids are home from school.

At five o'clock one hot June day on 100th Street that life began to grow. The women hung from the hundred faces of the windows, their breasts pressed against the sills, their eyes on the living street. In the vacant lot that looked like a bombed-out building site the small children romped across the dirt that glittered with broken glass, beneath the long-strung flags of washing — white, green, yellow, and red. Down the block the Pentecostal Church of *Espíritu Sanctu* beat its bass drum and made its call that comes whenever there are two or three to gather together in morning or afternoon or night. The men in slacks and sport shirts and open-neck white shirts sat, waiting on doorsteps, and stood beside doorways, leaning on buildings. The afternoon was hot and bright, and the sun made yellow shafts on the dark of the tenements.

A tall, dark man in a white shirt, a rust-colored cap on his head and a light brown jacket flung over one arm, stepped out of a doorway, looked each way down the street, and drew a large black wrench from under his jacket. He fitted it onto the top of the fire hydrant in the middle of the block, and twisted it. A silver stream came out of the hydrant, first in an arc, then thickened and straightened and shot across the street. The hissing sound it made grew as it widened and reached across the street, and was joined by the voices of the kids that grew around it. They ran from the vacant lot and out of doorways, dancing and yelling, and the man who had made the miracle — the silver water in a dry, dark land — stepped back into a knot of men and women, a smile across his face, his eyes fixed on the children. He slipped the wrench back under his jacket. Farther down the street the cry came to look — *"Mira, mira!"* The man with the wrench walked past the gusher, across the street to another doorway, watching the street from a different angle, smiling still, an artist appraising his work and finding it satisfactory.

A group of T-shirted boys had gathered at the hydrant, and one came running with an empty beer can whose ends were pushed out. The biggest of the boys knelt down behind the hydrant like a trapper of animals kneeling behind his prey, and fitted the can over the hydrant, over the silver stream, funneling it into the air, raising it to rain on the storefront window of the Baptist church across the street. The stream turned, writhed, and twisted, rose higher, the voices of the children rising with it, until the boy no longer had control and the can flew out of his hands and sailed through the air across to the other sidewalk.

A bony, tan boy in a skintight yellow bathing suit ran from a doorway and into the stream where the water hit the opposite curb and sprayed into white foam that flowed away in a small torrent that blackened with the street. The boy danced in the small spray, raising his feet as if the street were on fire. A boy on a bicycle sped toward the stream and streaked through it, and two more boys on bicycles followed. A barefoot girl tossed a tin can into the growing torrent at the curb. A new boy trapped the stream with a can and turned it skyward and a group of boys and girls ran under the high-falling spray, the hands and faces of the girls uplifted to catch it as it fell and cooled them. A boy lifted his pants above bright-striped socks and ran through the stream, his shoes sopping wet but his pants cuffs dry.

The yells of peoples' names and the exclamation of *"Mira!"* was suddenly interrupted by a different shout — *"Policía, policía!"* A boy from a window pointed toward First Avenue and a slowly striding, tall policeman, his face blank, his club swinging idly at his side. The kids dropped cans and ran and the stranger in blue brought his own wrench out and tightened the top of the hydrant. The gushing grew quiet, fizzed, drew in from its powerful stream across the street, became a small silver fountain poured on the curb, and died. The kids rushed around it and knelt below the mouth of the hydrant, holding up hands to catch the last drops of water. The stranger gave the final twist and the kids moved back, staring at where the life was, slowly scattering again to where they had been — marbles and baseball and doorsteps and glass-sprinkled empty lots of dust and garbage. Three bicycles returned, circling through the black surface of water still remaining, then they too moved on, pumping slowly, out of sight.

In several more hours the street will be dark, and the long, hot night of Harlem will begin. Within it, before it is broken with dawn, someone perhaps will remember the promise that made him come here and now has a different, more hopeless significance. This is New York and the long night's journey is not yet over and it still is no good to be poor.

The young children's group at the community center of the Good Neighbor Church on East 106th Street asked their teacher to take them again to Ward's Island, the small spot of green and uncluttered lawn that is just off the coast of the neighborhood in the East River. The teacher asked why they wanted to go there, and one of the kids explained that "we like to pretend that we're in a different world."

The World of the Spirits

Fifteen apparitions have I seen;
The worst a coat upon a coathanger . . .

— WILLIAM BUTLER YEATS

THE BELIEVERS in the spirits of the water had gathered at a ninth-floor apartment of the East River housing project to celebrate a feast of saints. A large, white cake with the names of the evening's honored spirits frosted on the top of it sat in the middle of a table laden with olives, cheese, and fruit. The living room's other furniture consisted of folding chairs for the guests, one large armchair in the corner, and a dressing table with a large mirror and a large collection of unopened bottles whose contents ranged from Puerto Rican rum to Old Mr. Boston Lemon-Flavored Gin. But in spite of the extra chairs, food, and drink brought in for the ceremonies, the room had the sense of bareness and transience that seems to come with the rooms of a project. There was no rug on the newly waxed floor, and its blank expanse, extended upward by the pale green walls, was not filled up but rather accentuated by the folding chairs that were the room's main furniture. A tape recorder (appropriately portable) sat in what seemed a precarious balance on one of the folding chairs by the wall. Out of it, sounding so full and therefore foreign to the room, came festive, rhythmic music, rich with guitars and choruses in Spanish.

María Flores had gone to the celebration with several friends, one of her daughters, and a deep respect for the work of the spirits, despite many scoffing denials of "really believing." María has said many times that "I just can't believe that stuff," though her parents believe, and she is glad they do — it has saved her daughter. María's oldest daughter had attacks of epilepsy at the age of nine, and María took her to several hospitals and they all said the child was incurable. The last doctor told María that her daughter's seizures would probably become more frequent, and she soon would have to be put in an institution. María told her parents what happened and they asked to take the girl to a medium for help.

"I couldn't take her myself because I didn't believe enough," María explained. "But my parents believe, and they took her to Ferina, every week, and in about six months she wasn't having the seizures nearly as much. I took her back to the doctors at the hospital and they said, 'What happened to this child?' Well, I wasn't going to tell them, but the only thing that happened was seeing Ferina. The doctor said she wouldn't have to be institutionalized after all. She still has the seizures sometimes, but she does go to school and lives with me and most of the time she's all right."

Ferina, the woman who had cured the child, was scheduled to be one of the mediums "working" at the celebration in the East River project. Like most of the water spirits' followers, Ferina is from Santo Domingo, one of the principal seats of the occult in the West Indies. The water spirits' rites are rarely practiced in Puerto Rico, where the spirits of the air or spirits of the white table are in great favor. But once in New York

— especially in Spanish Harlem — many Puerto Ricans attend the sessions of the spirits of the water. There is actually little difference in the basic beliefs and practices of the two sects, but rather in how they are carried out. The spirits of the air or white table followers look on the water sect as too wild, for the water services always include drinking, smoking, and a generally festive atmosphere.

A number of Puerto Ricans, including María and her friends, had come to the water spirits' feast at the East River project, though the host-family and most of the guests were from Santo Domingo. About eight-thirty the guests began to assemble on the folding chairs in the living room and sat, waiting, occasionally talking quietly among themselves as the two hostesses hurried back and forth from kitchen to living room to bedroom in preparation for the ceremonies. The lady of the house was a middle-aged, bright-eyed woman with jet-black hair pulled back to a knot in Indian fashion, and large, gold circular earrings that dangled from delicate chains. She greeted the guests, took their coats, and ushered the children to a room in the back where they could go if they were bored with the goings-on of the spirits. In all these matters the lady of the house was aided by her mother, a smiling, toothless, white-haired woman who scuffed about in men's leather bedroom slippers, her great bulk encircled by an apron whose decoration was a map of Ohio.

At about nine-thirty, when the living room was nearly filled with people, the tape recorder, which almost had reached the end of the tape, began playing "Ave Maria." There were many "shhhhs" for quiet, and the people stopped talking. The evening's rites were under way.

The lady of the house, a blue silk kerchief wrapped around

her head now, emerged from the kitchen with a pitcher of water. She went to the door of the apartment, which had just been locked, and faced upward to a picture above it of the nail-scarred hand of Christ. The water was lifted three times toward it while the guests in the living room watched in silence. After that offering, the hostess went to the table that was laden with food, banged the pitcher of water three times on top of it, and then let it rest there.

A rich, sweet odor came from the kitchen and a man with a thin, serious face and a thin mustache, a red kerchief wrapped around his neck, came out bearing a small urn that was burning incense. He gave it to the lady of the house, and she went to the door again to lift the urn, as she had the pitcher, three times upward to the hand of Christ. Then she wound her way through the guests in the living room, waving the incense past their faces, stopping to hold it for a moment in front of a large electric fan, while the air became thick and sweet. She set down the urn then and took from the dressing table in the living room one of the many bottles — but not of liquor. The bottle contained a clear, fragrant mixture called "Florida Water." The hostess poured a bit into the outstretched palm of each guest, and each one rubbed it into his hands and face.

In the only easy chair in the living room a huge, tan-faced woman had leaned back with her eyes closed when the "Ave Maria" began to play, and as the last of the guests were receiving the Florida Water she suddenly raised up, arms outstretched, and her body shook with a quick contortion. She sat upright in the chair, opened her eyes, and said, *"Buenos noches."* The room was silent as she spoke, and then in a low, reverent whisper, the words came back from the guests, in return: *"Buenos noches."* The greeting had not really come from the woman in the chair who spoke it, but rather from the spirit that now possessed her. Her body moved heavily forward in the chair. From a woman on her left who held an array of colored scarves and strings of beads she selected a pink scarf, wrapped it around her head, and reared up out of the chair to a standing position. One leg was several inches shorter than the other, and she moved across the room, all eyes on her, in a swaying walk that was almost a dance, her large brown eyes suddenly flashing to a face in the crowd, staring at it knowingly, and then passing on. This was Ferina, one of the most renowned of the women who "work" with the spirits of the water in Spanish Harlem.

Ferina went to each person in the room, one by one, and held out her hands. Each guest rose, extended the first finger of each of his own hands, and Ferina grasped them and crossed the person's arm twice, staring intently, then bowing in the sway with which she walked and passing on to the next. Several times, after crossing a guest, Ferina closed her eyes and placed her hands on the man or woman's head, as if in examination of some strange spirit. Her face would wrinkle in concentration, and her hands move delicately but firmly on the person's head, like the hands of a blind man examining a piece of sculpture. After several moments she would either frown and shake her head or smile with wisdom and satisfaction. The different attitudes revealed a great lack or great presence of receptivity to the spirits in the person who was being examined. With those who were lacking, Ferina's hands moved coldly, mutely upon their heads. With those who possessed great spiritual receptiveness, Ferina's hands and arms seemed to come alive. When she placed her hands on the head of María's daughter, it seemed as if the girl's black, tightly waved hair conducted an electric current into the hands and arms of the medium.

"You see," María whispered to a guest, "my girl is very receptive. She could 'work' with the spirits right now if I'd let her. She probably will when she gets a little older, but I hate to see it. It's dangerous."

The dangers involved in the world of the spirits soon became apparent, as Ferina moved toward a pale, pregnant girl with deep-grooved circles under her eyes who was sitting on a folding chair in the front row, staring straight ahead. As Ferina approached, the girl began to quiver. When Ferina took hold of her outstretched fingers both of the women's arms raised up, lowered, and stretched together in strange and violent gestures as if some power were controlling them both. When Ferina passed on, the pregnant girl covered her face with her hands. Her teeth chattered loudly and her breath came in spasms that occasionally broke in a sharp, painful hissing sound.

When every person in the room had been crossed by Ferina (those who came later were crossed before being seated) she returned to the easy chair in the corner and fell back into it, closing her eyes. Her body jerked forward and shook with spasms, and her arms reached out as if just about to grasp some elusive revelation, only to drop back again, accompanied by a heavy sigh. Suddenly Ferina leaned forward, uttered a cry, a laugh, and fell back just as quickly into what seemed a coma. The guests looked on in a hushed, anxious expectancy, hardly moving. Ferina slowly sat forward in her chair, opened her eyes, and announced that nothing much had come from the spirit who had just been in possession of her — at least "nothing important."

The guests relaxed, began to talk among themselves, and a sort of recess set in. But there was no recess for the spirits. A black-skinned young girl with full lips and a proud, erect body began to quiver and moved back and forth in her chair in a shivering transport that grew increasingly more intense and ended with her flinging her earrings off, lying back, opening her eyes, and smiling peacefully. The hostess came over and gave her a colored handkerchief that is worn by all who "work" — that is, those who are able to be possessed by the spirits.

In the meantime Ferina had fallen back into another coma, and awoke this time to remove her pink handkerchief and wrap a new scarlet one around her head and a green one around her waist. The changing of one colored handkerchief for another means that a new spirit has entered the medium. The red and green combination are the colors of an especially fun-loving spirit who was, in his time on earth, a prominent African king. Ferina, who is known in the neighborhood when not possessed as a mild and abstinent woman who neither smokes nor drinks, swayed to the mirrored table and lit up a monstrous White Owl cigar. The gentleman assistant with the kerchief around his neck hurried to the bedroom and brought out a scarlet robe with gold sequins that Ferina slipped on over her dress. She held up her arms and swayed in a dance to the music on the tape recorder, snapping her fingers and grinning broadly. She called to the assistant again and he handed her a fifth of rum from the table, which she opened and pressed to her mouth, leaning backward to pour down a giant-sized swig. It is said that those possessed by the spirits may drink all they wish and not become affected by the alcohol. It is not the body of the person, but the visiting spirit inside the body that consumes the liquor. Ferina, many swigs later in the evening, careened about the room in a steadily progressive loss of her swaying balance, but this was attributed to the spirit (rather than the spirits) inside her at the time.

The spirit having taken a drink, it was now permissible for guests to have a drink. The mustached man with the red kerchief came from the kitchen with a tray of bright-colored paper cups inscribed with the message "Happy Birthday" and filled with beer. As the guests drank and talked among themselves Ferina moved about the room, a bulky but agile spirit, the long cigar clenched defiantly in her mouth, tilting upward as she stopped to appraise a guest and stare toward the ceiling, suddenly speaking some hidden information concerning family, lover, or friend. Each person nodded when given information, smiling in satisfied wonder as Ferina ended the revelation with a confident *"Tu sabe?"* (You know?); and they always knew.

Ferina's face fell into ominous frowns as she stopped in front of several guests who watched and waited in frozen anxiety, only to have the spirit move on in silence. Dark information was given only to the pregnant girl, whose pale face fixed in stiff and stoic attention on Ferina, who said that some person in the girl's apartment building was trying to destroy her with a spell.

The pregnant girl indeed seemed possessed. She fell into spasms and trances throughout the evening, sometimes not moving from her chair but throwing her arms up in front of her face as if in protection from an unseen, cosmic enemy of the highest order. Once as Ferina moved blithely back and forth, the pregnant girl began to shiver and breathe in hissing spasms with a special intensity, and suddenly flung herself out of her seat and began to careen around the room. Her arms waved wildly and her body shook with deep convulsions that became a kind of frenzied dance that hardly fitted the festive guitar music playing on the tape recorder. She stopped and opened her eyes in front of a guest and began to speak, rapidly but clearly, trying with controlled desperation to relay the message before it was too late. She moved from person to person down the row, extending her vibrating hand to press their foreheads and spill forth a message of past or future significance to them. She stopped in front of a sallow-faced, middle-aged woman who had recently experienced a great family crisis, and told her that the trial was about to pass, and its passing could be hastened by taking a bath in certain herbs. A handsome man in the row behind, nattily dressed in a blue sport coat, yellow slacks, and black and white wing-tipped shoes, had been looking on with a faintly amused and casual air, but when the formula of herbs was recited he hastily reached in his pocket and drew forth a pencil and a piece of paper. He pressed them into the hand of the woman in front, and she hurriedly recorded the proper ingredients to mix for the bath of her predicted salvation. Instructions such as these must be written down at once, for they come not from the medium but the spirit in possession, and once the spirit has gone the instructions are gone too, and the medium will not know what they were.

The pregnant woman, shivering constantly the whole time she spoke, progressed down the row for revelations to seven people. After the seventh message she turned away, heading for her chair, but being possessed with frightening violence, threw herself (or was thrown, according to the eye of the beholder) onto the floor and writhed there, flailing her arms and legs as people moved their chairs back, silently watching and moving chairs and feet from the path of her contortions. A man in the back row who was new to the sessions jumped up and asked that someone stop her. He was quickly subdued while the rest of the guests remained in their seats and the blue-kerchiefed lady of the house calmly picked up a small red bell and tinkled it rapidly, giving sign to the spirit to subside. The woman possessed eventually slowed her flailing and rose, alone, to return to her seat where she clutched her head in her hands, breathing heavily. Finally she lowered her hands and stared ahead with her pale face calm in the smile of a saint who is at peace in the perfect conviction of her faith.

No one else was touched with the violence of the pregnant woman's experience. Ferina went about her work with the easy enjoyment and almost relaxed convulsions of the old pro, and was felt by the guests to be the most successful of those who "worked" — as was expected.

Others of the guests periodically rose in the frenzy of possession, the neighbors sitting around them showing no sign of surprise, but calmly picking up the earrings or scarves that were tossed in the seizure of the spirit to hold until the return of the body to the quiet pose it had been in before. The only difference after the experience was found in the perfect smile that divides the select from the mass of men, and contains both relief for having been chosen and a terrible pity for those who are blind. Only the seized individuals rose from their chairs, and possession or its aid was the only reason for a person moving from his seat through the seven hours of the spirits' reign.

The spirits were gracious enough to subside from strenuous activity at approximately hour intervals when food or drink was passed around. After the beer were shots of whiskey, roast beef sandwiches, rum, gin, cheese, olives, birthday cake, and more beer. After each particular course was finished, one spirit or other would faithfully return to seize some person present and begin a new pattern of possession and revelation, bringing the believers advice and signs of affirmation from the other world as well as hope for this one. Through the dark window the far-flung lights of the world outside — going about its business, unknowing — shone as a sparkling image, but hardly seemed anything more than that; hardly seemed more than a decoration set in the face of this inner world so crowded with the spirits of the dead and the hopes of the living.

The hopes of the living in Spanish Harlem are focused on the spirits of the dead to a deep degree. A businessman who set up his office in the neighborhood was surprised to find that one of the men who worked for him — a fellow he supposed was a Catholic — had put up some bells above the door of the office to bring the luck and blessing of the spirits. The newcomer asked a suave, second-generation native of the neighborhood if this fellow actually "believed in spiritualism." The native smiled and said, "If you ever talk to a Puerto Rican who says he doesn't believe in the spirits, you know what that means? It means you haven't talked to him long enough."

The newcomer was quiet for a moment and asked, "Does this mean you too?"

The friend smiled again and said, "Well, I have heard some things. I have seen some things. I wouldn't deny them."

Denials often come at first in conversations with outsiders who obviously are nonbelievers, but the neighborhood maxim that you just have to talk to a Puerto Rican long enough to see that he believes is a pretty sound rule. There are many like María Flores, who begins by saying she doesn't believe and ends by telling how the spirits saved her daughter.

Testimony is everywhere. It is found — though not as easily — among the local dignitaries, who often go to great pains to hide their belief. A group made up of doctors, lawyers, and businessmen from Spanish Harlem go to spiritualist meetings at a place in midtown Manhattan in order not to be seen at this practice by the people of the neighborhood.

There are many community stories told of how Tony Mendez, the owner of a local jewelry store and head of the Caribe Club (Tammany Hall's Spanish Harlem branch) often calls upon the spirits for help but tries to keep it a secret. One of the stories is that Tony's wife, Isabel, once was invited to attend a session of the spirits in the neighborhood, and, thinking it was to be private, accepted the invitation for herself and her husband. When she learned that a large group of people from the neighborhood were going to be there, she said that she and her husband would not be able to come.

Belief in the works of the spirits is by no means restricted, as is sometimes said, to the poor or uneducated, among either the Puerto Ricans of New York City or those on the island. Although they may preface their remarks with a statement of personal nonbelief, the story that follows is usually a tale of testimony. Hipolito Marcano, a well-known member of the Puerto Rican senate and head of the Masonic Lodge of Puerto Rico, told a visitor the story of a man from San Juan who became a painter through the help and direction of the spirits. It seems that this man, who never in his life had been interested in art, attended a spiritualist meeting on the mainland and was told by a spirit to take up painting. The man returned to San Juan, bought himself a brush and a palette, and went to work. He went on to establish a solid, if not sensational, reputation as a local painter and did a large portrait of the former Puerto Rican labor leader, Santiago Iglesias, which hangs in one of the government buildings of the island.

A few days after Mr. Marcano told this story, the visitor who heard it was standing at the San Juan airport with a man as different in personality and formal religion from Hipolito Marcano as anyone could wish to find. Frank Ruiz, the grizzled former truckdriver who is secretary-treasurer of the Sugar Workers Union, wears a silver St. Christopher's medal that hangs out over a short-sleeved open-neck sport shirt that hangs out over his pants, and he presents altogether an opposite image from that of the stately, senatorial, Protestant Mr. Marcano. Ruiz was discussing the seasonal migration of workers to the mainland when he stopped, nudged his visitor, and pointed to a well-dressed gentleman who was walking by the airport ticket counter.

"You see that man?" said Ruiz. "That is an interesting story. That man went to the states to a spiritualist conference and was told to take up painting. Well, he had never painted in his life and he wasn't a young man, but he came back home and started painting. He painted the picture of Santiago Iglesias that is very well known here."

The story was told by both men without any personal comment, but rather a tone of "Take it or leave it — but there it is."

"There it is" throughout the fabric of Puerto Rican life, whether on the island or the mainland. It is, in fact, one of the main, continuous threads that ties that life together. The closest that a Puerto Rican in the asphalt jungle of Spanish

Harlem can come to the particular essence of his tropical island home is the session that calls forth the spirits of the other
world — a world that knows no problems of migration and
sends it messengers with equal ease to San Juan or New
York City.

The world of the spirits has been historically the most private world of the Puerto Ricans in the face of the always en-
croaching worlds of invaders from Spain and then from
America. It has happened by both desire and necessity, for
both the Spanish and Americans brought to the island religions and rules that were different from and in fact officially
opposed to the practice of the spirits. That practice had to go
underground, and the people had to keep it and its life in secret while keeping another religious life in the shrines and
churches imported by strangers. This was the necessity for
more than four hundred years of Spanish rule, and the habit
has made it the case even now, sixteen hundred miles from the
island in New York City, where the Puerto Ricans still, in the
great majority, go to a Catholic or perhaps a Protestant
church on the street and practice the work of the spirits behind the closed doors of a private home. Spiritualism (as well
as Protestantism) was outlawed in Puerto Rico during the
Spanish rule, and the private practice with the spirits was condemned by the Bishop of San Juan in the following specific
terms:

> We reiterate the prohibition against assistance at sessions,
> against consultation of media and curers, even when they
> clothe themselves in a pious air, due to the great danger
> which spiritualist practices . . . hold for the faith.

The church also outlawed the saint cults, which blended
Catholicism with African and Indian beliefs by "adopting" a

particular saint, giving it a special name based on some characteristic of the saint's appearance or history (the church's prohibition forbade giving saints "exotic" names), calling upon it for special favors and working out special rituals of thanks and request. The kind of practice worked out by these cults is typified in the custom of some of them of dipping an image of the saint in water to bring about rain.

The constant blending of religions and cultures continued in spite of all edicts, and went on within the world of the spirits as well as through the practice of the saint cults. The results of this process of mixture and absorption was displayed at the celebration of the spirits of the water at the East River housing project, which wove into one evening's ritual experience the playing of "Ave Maria," the offering of a pitcher of water three times before the hand of Christ, the presence (as indicated by the color of handkerchiefs worn by the medium) of the spirit of a long-dead African king, and prescriptions of herbs for fending off evil.

Even the most private world of the Puerto Ricans is a world invaded by the cultures of the strangers, for although the native islanders kept the outsiders from the secret practice of the spirits, they brought to that practice hunks and pieces of the rulers' imported religion. The Puerto Ricans' private world of the spirits is, like all of their culture, a mixed and many-sided world.

In bringing it into the strange new streets of New York they have also brought the old fears that were once appropriate to it during the Spanish rule on the island. When the ceremony began in the East River project in the year of 1957, the door was locked and guests who came late were first checked through the small metal peephole that opens from inside before being admitted. When asked about this secrecy, one of the guests explained that practicing the work of the spirits outside of a church is "illegal" and that everyone might be arrested. There is of course no New York statute forbidding work with the spirits, but the long illegality of it on the island has maintained the necessity of secrecy as part of the practice.

The secrecy of a whole section of the Puerto Ricans' religious life, and the mixture and combinations of religious practice, has led to a great many false impressions in the outside world. Most often the Puerto Ricans are considered by people of the mainland as "naturally" being Catholics — as the Irish are "naturally" Catholics — and are shocked to hear that they are actually "spiritualists." But neither assumption is accurate. Most often they are neither one thing nor the other but both — or maybe both and more.

Most Puerto Ricans seem to have a marvelous, immense capacity for religion. Ramón Diaz, the adult director of a teen-age club in Spanish Harlem, is a whole appendix in himself to William James's *Varieties of Religious Experience*. Ramón was baptized a Catholic, came from the island to the mainland on a Bahai pilgrimage, joined the East Harlem Protestant Parish, and attends the private sessions of the spirits. He, like nearly every other Puerto Rican, sees nothing contradictory or strange in devotion to different religions at the same time. Ramón is an honest man, and he is faithful to all. Why shouldn't he be? They all have different functions and serve different purposes. As María Flores explained her view of these functions, "You go to the Catholic church to get baptized and married and have the last rites." For day-to-day hopes and fears, however, the contact with the spirits of the dead and their specific cures and revelations seems more the answer. There are many in the neighborhood who take an active part in community activities of the Protestant churches, belong to the Catholic church, and attend spiritualist sessions in the homes of friends.

Work with the spirits is most often a private affair at home, and the number of people who belong to or even attend the formal services of storefront spiritualist churches in Spanish Harlem is very small in comparison. In the research volume, *The Puerto Rican Journey*, done by C. Wright Mills and a staff of Columbia University sociologists in 1948, it was reported that in percentage of church membership of Puerto Ricans in New York City "there is a thin stratum — about 2 per cent — of Spiritualists." This was of course the number claiming formal membership in the Spiritualist church, and probably has not changed. The consistently small percentage of Puerto Rican members of the Spiritualist church is often a misleading figure to outside observers who assume that the Puerto Ricans conduct their religious life by the same rules and rituals as, say, Irish Catholics or midwestern Protestants.

Formal membership and regular attendance in a Spiritualist church makes it much more difficult to keep up membership in a Catholic or Protestant church, and that is one of the several reasons it is not as desirable as private home sessions. There is actually little difference, though, between the beliefs and practices of the work with the spirits in the home or in the Puerto Rican Spiritualist church. All of the Puerto Rican Spiritualist churches in Spanish Harlem are followers of the white table or spirits of the air belief, which is also practiced widely in private sessions. This is the more conservative group, which does not allow food or drink at its ceremonies. The participants seat themselves around a table covered by a white cloth, with a pitcher of water in the center of it. Just as in the sessions of the spirits of the water, anyone present may "work" or be possessed by the spirits, and information is transferred through the medium to most of the people present. There are many groups in the neighborhood made up of mutual friends who meet for this purpose regularly, often once a week, in one of the friends' apartment. It is also common that people who are not in a regular group of this sort may arrange a meeting when someone is in need of help or advice and summon the aid of the spirits.

The followers of the spirits of the water hold their ceremonies according to fixed dates of celebration for principal spirits of their own belief. Distinctions between the water and air spirits are difficult to delineate — believers in each type become quite vague after naming one or two characteristics. The main differences seem to follow the basic attitudes of abstinence and indulgence that mark the spirits of the air and water respectively in their policies of eating and drinking during their ceremonies. The water spirits, who demand a good time when they make earthly contact, seem to be more demanding in every way than the milder, abstinent spirits of the air. And their reputation of having special power enables them to make the demands. The regular follower of the spirits of the air, who has also been to many water spirits sessions, describes the difference in this way:

"The water spirits are more likely to ask a price for their work. They do that by telling you, through the medium, to pay something to the medium or sometimes to a third party. Sometimes they ask you to burn a candle in their honor, or give them things to eat and drink — through the medium they're working in. But you see, even though you have to do these things sometimes — and a lot of people don't like that — the water spirits work much faster. They get things done much quicker than the air spirits can, and you can be more sure of something really happening."

Even in the world of the spirits, you get what you pay for. For those who are anxious to have something happen, there are in addition to the group sessions many mediums who work in private — for a fee, usually not more than five dollars a session. They bring advice, warning, and help in fighting off trouble caused by spirits hostile to the customer. The latter function is extremely important, for there are in the neighborhood — and back on the island as well — people who practice *brujería* (witchcraft). A *bruja*, or witch, is a person who is able and willing to use his gifts as a medium to summon up spirits for evil purposes. The spirits both of the air and of the water can be called into doing harm by a *bruja* and it takes another medium to undo the spell — if, indeed, it can be undone at all. There is a man on 102nd Street who is said to make his living from fees charged for working *brujería*. He does not ask the fee until the job has been done. If it has, there is hardly any question of the customer trying to welch on whatever fee is asked. The price of not paying, determined by the *bruja*, is too dark and terrible to contemplate.

There are many ways in which a person who wants to work *brujería* on an enemy can use special tricks to help him cast a spell. There is, for instance, a custom at Puerto Rican funerals for all the mourners to pick up a handful of dirt and toss it on the grave of the deceased before it is totally covered over. If one of the mourners takes a handful of dirt and pretends to toss it on the grave, but actually puts it in his pocket, he can use it later to help him summon the dead man's spirit for whatever sort of work he wishes — including the work of *brujería*.

But besides these special methods, there are for the normal work of casting spells and counterspells a whole stock of easily purchased materials — herbs, oils, candles, sprays, incense, bath salts, bells, and images. These can be bought at the small stores known as *Botánicas* that are found all through the streets of Spanish Harlem, often two and sometimes three on the same block. Their windows hold a deep, if often dusty, promise of miracles and cures. A typical *Botánica* on 114th Street contained in its window at the same time the following materials: Lady Luck Room Spray (*Roció Dama de Suerte*), Money-Drawing Room Spray, Jinx-Removing Deodorant Air Spray, Commanding Incense, Money-Drawing Incense, Holy Spirit Bath, Crusader Religious Candles, Magnetic St. Christopher's Statue, and a book entitled *How to Get Your Winning Number*. A few doors down the street, Rendon's *Botánica* — one of the oldest and most well known of these shops — displayed a house product of promise for a more customarily advertised mainland miracle, Rendon's Hair Application. The more effective and important herbs and oils are inside the shop, arranged like medicines, and purchased on prescription of the spirits themselves. The customers come out bearing them in brown-wrapped packages, accompanied by the slight tinkle of the bells that hang above nearly all *Botánica* doorways to bring the luck of the other world.

That luck is needed often in the slums of New York, and many Puerto Rican clergymen who have lived on both the island and the mainland feel that if anything there is more work with spirits among the migrants than the islanders. The

Reverend Rafael Cotto, minister of the Spanish-speaking congregation of the Protestant Church of the Good Neighbor on East 106th Street, says that "there seems to be more spiritualist practice here than on the island. There's a lot more of the 'business' side of it here, too; more of going to someone and paying and then having to go buy herbs and waters."

There is no way to measure accurately the increase in spiritualist interest among the migrants, but the many *Botánica*-studded streets of Spanish Harlem, as well as the neighborhood legends and rumors, bear testimony to its great importance. If there is actually the heightened interest in spiritualism that there seems to be among the migrants, it has a revealing correlation to importance of the spirits in different parts of the island itself. A group of anthropologists from Illinois University, who made an exhaustive study of the island culture in *The People of Puerto Rico*, found that the impact of spiritualist beliefs "seems to be greater in communities which are now undergoing comparatively rapid cultural change . . ." and among groups "which are losing or have recently lost their traditional way of life . . ."

But although the threat to traditional ways of life seems to stimulate a heightened interest in the spirits, that interest does not extend to regular, formal church activity. The findings of many church and university surveys have shown that a far fewer number of Puerto Ricans attend church services and keep up church ties in New York than on the island. This has been of special concern to the Catholic Church, which has a membership of roughly 85 per cent of the people in Puerto Rico. Although Catholicism has a four-century history on the island it is in many ways a history of conflict, and many problems of current Catholic efforts to hold the Puerto

Ricans to the faith in New York were planted long ago on the island by the old conquistadors. Bishoprics were established in Puerto Rico in 1511, but the priests were few in number and often were met with hostility. Ecclesiastical patronage was under the jurisdiction of the king of Spain, and the priest was the agent of the state as well as the church. Since the state was regarded as invader and oppressor, the native islanders often regarded the priests in the same way. Anticolonial sentiment was often developed into anti-Catholic sentiment, and some of the principal anti-colonial movements on the island were sponsored by secret Protestant religious movements. The islanders' regard of the church as a colonial force was further strengthened by the fact that Spain would only allow priests from Spain to work in Puerto Rico, for fear that native Puerto Rican priests would be natural leaders and potential organizers of revolutionary movements. As a result of that policy laid down four hundred years ago, Father Ivan Illich was writing in *The Commonweal* Magazine in 1956 of the Puerto Rican migrants in New York City that:

> The new arrival from Puerto Rico was not the Christian in his own right who received the faith from some of his own neighbors, but the fruit of missionary labor typical of the Spanish empire. He was a Catholic, born of parents who were also Catholics, yet he received the sacraments from a foreigner because the government was afraid that to train native priests might be to train political rebels.

The Catholic Church now is working to change that, and Puerto Rican native priests are found today both on the island and in New York. The problem of holding the migrants to the faith has caused great concern, for not only did many just drift away when they got to New York, but many were converted to different religions. The growth of Catholic churches, agencies, and studies established to reverse that trend has increased tremendously, especially within the last decade. In 1919 there were only two Catholic churches holding services in Spanish in New York, and by 1958 there were nearly fifty. In 1951 the Catholic Charities set up a branch in Spanish Harlem, and a year later a Catholic Spanish radio hour was born. A Spanish Catholic Action group was organized, which began its work by arranging education conferences for Puerto Ricans in the city, and holding a mass in honor of San Juan in New York's St. Patrick's Cathedral.

But as Catholic efforts to hold the Puerto Ricans have stepped up greatly, so have Protestant efforts to convert them. A Catholic estimate in the mid-1950's said that two hundred Protestant churches in New York City had some sort of program for proselytizing the Puerto Ricans. The first Protestant group to work in this direction on the mainland was the New York City Mission Society, which organized the First Spanish Evangelical Church in 1912. It moved six times as the main center of Puerto Rican settlement moved, and is today in East Harlem at 106th and Lexington, and is called now The Church of the Good Neighbor. The Reverend Herbert Yates, one of its ministers, made a study of the five Spanish-speaking churches sponsored by the New York City Mission Society, and came up with findings that confirm the Catholics' fears:

A large majority of first generation Puerto Ricans now in City Mission churches came directly from Roman Catholic backgrounds. The estimates of the ministers ranged from

75% to 90%. The influence of this background varies among the churches from one extreme to another. In one church all vestiges of Roman Catholic worship have been eliminated, and there is a strong emphasis on Biblical Evangelical preaching (a typical reaction among Latin American Evangelicals). In another there were people who still keep religious medals and pictures in their homes. At least one of the ministers expressed the desire to see more formal worship services and more beautiful sanctuaries for Puerto Rican Protestants. Many of the people have relatives who are Catholics, and this is not infrequently a source of friction for them.

This has also caused problems for the churches of the East Harlem Protestant Parish, whose extensive youth program draws great numbers of boys and girls whose families are not otherwise involved in the church, and often are Catholics. It sometimes happens that Catholic parents forbid the children to take part in the Parish youth activities, even though they may not be religious activities.

When the men and women of the Parish first moved into East Harlem with a single storefront church in 1948, they had almost every strike against them. Nearly all of them were white. Nearly all of them spoke only English. The great majority of the residents in their parish were at least nominal Catholics. And yet, in the first decade of its existence, the Parish grew to four churches with a group ministry of fifteen men and women, a total membership of more than five hundred, and a program that reached an estimated two thousand people in the neighborhood throughout the year. The Parish and its many activities has become an integral part of the neighborhood, despite the obstacles it started with. Whatever its strictly religious impact has been in this world of the spirits, Pentecostal revivals, and Catholic masses, it has without question become the greatest social force in the neighborhood. However, a statement explaining its aims and work that the Parish itself has put out says that "evangelism is our total and only reason for being in East Harlem." To a person who has lived in the neighborhood and witnessed the variety of Parish activities, ranging from help for narcotics addicts to street-gang work, this seems a misleading statement. But few groups or persons ever define themselves very clearly to the outside world when they set out to do it. A far better insight into the spirit and success of the Parish can be found in a letter from the Reverend George Todd, one of its ministers, written in reply to a debate on the church and juvenile delinquency in the magazine, *Christianity and Crisis:*

. . . The church cannot be satisfied to put up an "Everybody Welcome" sign and be happy if a few Negro or Puerto Rican children find their way into the Sunday school. One church school teacher said to me: "We have no prejudice in our Sunday School. We have six Negro children from the neighborhood in our membership. They are the cleanest, most well-behaved children you could hope to meet." The church must look outside its doors at those who appear to be dirty, disruptive, and unattractive and recognize them to be the very ones for whom the church exists. No Sunday School or youth fellowship program, no group work or case work program can substitute for a community of Christians who are willing to expose themselves and their church by living with and loving the most troubled youth of a parish.

In a community or city where thousands upon thousands of young people do not know a wholesome home life, do not enjoy the kinds of material things they see in ads and movies, do not experience an ordered community life, it is irrelevant for a church to devise a program based on the aim of improving the moral standards of young people. In East Harlem, for instance, forces stronger than any individual or institution have a powerful hold on children growing up in a context of life devoid of what the church has thought of as normative, "respectable" morality. Think of:

A girl, who wasn't wanted by her mother in the first place, who has seen her mother living with several men, who has never known her father, and who has no resources or reasons for resisting the offer of affection which leaves her carrying a child who will know even less of the pattern of what we call Christian family life.

A boy, whose father is a drunkard and thief and whose mother is a prostitute, and who finds recognition at home from what he can steal. A 17-year-old girl, whose mother left "for a week or so" with a boy friend, is left with three small children to care for and goes out of her mind. A boy, whose father is a hopeless TB case and whose mother is mentally unstable, tries to forget his expulsion from school for bad behavior by taking heroin.

Christ was mocked for making merry and for breaking bread with sinners. The Body of Christ, his church, must know, accept and share in the life of young people who drink, use narcotics, steal, have out-of-wedlock sex experience, dance the "fish" and the "grind," carry guns and knives, are truants or have quit school, and who do not hold jobs. Their alienation from the church, from society, from all men is great. They desperately crave love and affection and acceptance even though they are not able to accept it when it is offered. They need to have it offered again and again . . .

The church does not exist to keep its membership pure from such as are called juvenile delinquents, nor does it exist to keep its property in first-rate condition. The church is the Body of Christ set in the middle of the world to give its life away that men might know the good news of a God who loves them.

One church stopped calling on youth in a new low-income public housing project after some of the young people came to a youth group meeting in response to visits from the church staff. In a scuffle, a church chandelier was damaged and a wall was marred. "We can't have youth who don't know how to behave without breaking up our nice group," one of the leaders said. This church with its upholstered furniture, grand pianos, and stained glass windows might yet discover that God would bless it in its true vocation if it were to make the youth of its parish welcome there, even though it might mean names scratched on spotless walls and broken panes in the stained glass. Youth who never saw love in action have to test it for a long time before they believe it . . .

The message of the letter conveys far better than any of its official statements the place and importance of the Parish in the neighborhood. Its work has been great, and its storefront churches have become as much a part of East Harlem as the candy stores and butcher shops they replaced on the streets. But it cannot be said that the religious life of the Parish has stirred a great movement to the Protestant faith among the Puerto Ricans of East Harlem — any more than any traditional Protestant movements have stirred such an appeal among Puerto Ricans, either in New York or on the island. The Parish, as well as the Spanish congregations sponsored by the New York City Mission Society, has to rely on outside funds for its continued work. The Parish did raise $13,000 from the neighborhood itself in one year, but it is principally supported by donations from eight different Protestant denominations as well as the New York City Mission. The only completely self-supporting Protestant religious sect among the Puerto Ricans is the only Protestant sect that has naturally

flourished both on the island and in Spanish Harlem — that is
the Protestant "fringe" sect known as Pentecostal, which is
looked upon as heretic by the other traditional or "ecumenical" Protestant faiths. The Pentecostals pose the greatest
challenge to both Catholic and traditional Protestant movements in attracting Puerto Ricans. The Pentecostals in fact
are so strong that they also present a threat — which no other
formal religious group seriously does — to the practice of
spiritualism.

Protestants have estimated that the total Protestant strength
in Puerto Rico is 200,000, but of that number only 50,000 are
members of traditional Protestant churches. The rest are part
of the growing groups that are mainly called Pentecostal and
also include titles such as Church of Christ, Adventist, and
Holiness, and are nearly identical in program and fervor. The
phenomenon of the Pentecostal strength is especially amazing
because of the fact that they are the latest recruiters to come
on the scene.

When the U.S. took Puerto Rico from Spain in 1898 the
island was for the first time opened to Protestant proselytizing. The Protestant churches, anxious to make the most of the
opportunity and waste as few resources as possible, divided
the island like a large pie and assigned slices to various de-
nominations. The Methodists got the north, the Baptists a
sliver across the middle, the Presbyterians a hunk in the west,
and so forth. It was agreed that the groups would work
solely within their own sections so they wouldn't be battling
among themselves. One bizarre by-product of this pie system
was explained by a native Puerto Rican in this way:

"If a man is a Protestant, you can usually tell what part of
the island he's from. If he's a Methodist, he must be from

Arecibo; a Baptist is probably from Ponce — you usually can tell."

The one Protestant sect that doesn't fit the pattern is the Pentecostal. They were not in on the original division of the Protestant pie, and did not in fact get into the act until the 1930's. It is a measure of their swift success among the Puerto Ricans that a man who is a Pentecostal may be from anywhere on the island; the Pentecostals are everywhere. This has failed to bring joy to the hearts of "regular" Protestants, however, any more than it has to the Catholics, or even the spiritualists — to anyone, for that matter, except the Pentecostals, who seem to be happier than all the rest.

The discovery of their power and appeal has come as a shock to many orthodox Protestant leaders. In the 1950's the president of Union Theological Seminary, Henry Van Dusen, took a holiday to the Caribbean and found that his troops were being pressed to the wall on every front by the Pentecostal "fringe sects." Dr. Van Dusen had met this menace before, in a trip around the world, where he found that in talking with Protestant leaders almost everywhere — Asia, Japan, Pakistan, the Gold Coast — ". . . the problem thrust before me as their most pressing and baffling present harassment was always the same — the pressure of these 'fringe sects.' "

And, on his Caribbean holiday, Dr. Van Dusen found more of the same:

"My principal discovery, though not altogether new, was the third mighty arm of Christian outreach, standing on the opposite side of traditional Protestantism from Roman Catholicism — that whole vast complex of groups of Christian allegiance bearing in their titles the designation 'Adventist' or

'Pentecostal' or 'Holiness' or simply 'Church of God' or 'Church of Christ' — the groups of which we speak, when we trouble to note them at all, as 'fringe sects.' "

And just what is this thunder on the fringe? Dr. Van Dusen described the principal characteristics of these sects as follows:

"Spiritual ardor, sometimes but by no means always with excessive emotionalism; immediate experience of the living Christ, sometimes with aberrations; intimate and sustaining fellowships, sometimes with excesses; leading of the Holy Spirit, sometimes but not always with exaggerated claims; intense apocalypticism . . . but hardly more extreme than what is the current vogue in some segments of respectable contemporary ecumenical Protestantism; above all, a life-commanding, life-transforming, seven days a week devotion, however limited in outlook, to a living Lord of all life."

One thinks of the New Testament.

What Dr. Van Dusen describes as "respectable ecumenical Protestantism" has suffered the same "baffling harassment" by the Christian fringe sects in New York City, especially among the Puerto Ricans. In Spanish Harlem the Pentecostal store-front churches are almost as numerous as the *Botánicas*. Some of them are open every night; some in the afternoon.

One hot summer evening on 109th Street east of Fifth Avenue the blue and orange neon cross that spelled in Spanish the name of the Pentecostal church was the only bright spot on the block. It was Sunday night, and the people of the neighborhood leaned from dimly lit windows and sat on the steps of dark buildings. Out of the street's two directions of darkness small groups of men and women and children, dressed in their finest, came toward the cross, sometimes stopping to talk before entering the large, arching doors that opened on the deep light and sound of the service inside. A young girl strange to the block walked east from Fifth Avenue down 108th Street, and slowed as she neared the church.

"*Habla español?*"

A sallow-faced, smiling man with a large black megaphone hanging from his neck moved from the front of the church toward the girl to hail her with a handful of leaflets. His eyes were bright behind thick, steel-rimmed glasses, although they were shadowed not only by the night but also by a dark green celluloid eyeshade of the type once common to copy-desk men. He touched his thumb to his tongue and peeled off one of the leaflets from his stack, starting to talk before the girl had a chance to read it. He asked if she was *Católica* and she said no, she belonged to the Protestant Church of the Good Neighbor, on 106th Street.

The man gave a smile of tolerance and wondered if the girl understood that the Pentecostal church was now "the church of power."

"The other churches," he explained before she could answer, "have no power, and that is what is needed now. In former times those churches like the Presbyterians, Episcopalians, they were all right — but not any more. The weight of sin on the country is much too great for them now. Billy Graham — did you hear Billy Graham — he is right, he says this country will either be saved or destroyed. He is saved himself, that's how he can preach like that, say those things he says. A man who wasn't saved couldn't say those things. He is doing right. But the other Protestant faiths, they may want to, but they don't have the power any more. The Pentecostal church, you know, has the power to heal — and that's what it says in the Bible, those with faith are able to heal the sick. I have heard of many wonders — seen people who threw away their crutches and went out of hospitals healed by the Pentecostal faith. That is the true faith.

"You know," the man asked rhetorically, "why it is we have the true faith?

"Because," he answered himself, "we live by the faith — live by it strictly. A member here cannot smoke or drink or be divorced. The members are tithed, but only the members — other people pay no tithe, are not allowed to. Sometimes the members fail to live by the faith and cannot be members any longer. They still can come to the church, worship here, but not as members. You see, it has gotten so even the Catholic *priests* now smoke — but we do not even have members who smoke. We live by the faith and have power from it.

"And did you know," the man asked, his voice rising in the joy of belief, "that the Pentecostal church has stopped Communism in South America? That takes power. The other faiths don't have that much. The power of the Pentecostal church is the strongest thing against Communism. Look at China. The faiths there were weak, and the Christian missionaries had not enough power — there were no Pentecostal churches there — and what happened? The Communists took over. Took over all China, and now it is too late there. But other places the Pentecostal church is the only answer, and the only real strength against Communists."

A loudspeaker attached to the second floor of the church began to crackle, and filled the air outside with Spanish. The girl, looking up, remarked that the church was a very nice one. It was made of gray stone, with high stained-glass windows.

"Yes," the man with the megaphone smiled, "we bought it about ten years ago from the Jews. It used to be a synagogue. We also bought another one from them up the street. This one we bought just after the war, about ten years ago I think."

Spirited music had begun to blare from the speaker, and the girl asked if she might go in. The recruiter stretched out his arm toward the door, his face glistening with perspiration beneath the green eyeshade. He watched, still smiling, as she entered, then hiked up his trousers that were held in place by wide blue suspenders, and walked again toward the curb, the megaphone swinging at his waist as he went, squinting into the night.

Inside, the girl walked up the stairs to the main floor, and was guided to a seat on the left side of the church, where a sign on the wall read *Damas*. On the opposite side was a sign that said *Caballeros*, signifying the place for the men. There were actually three rows of pews, the men filling the one to the right and women filling the other two. There was no sign or specific place for *los niños*, but the children were everywhere — sitting on the laps of fathers, lying in the arms of mothers, walking casually up and down the aisles, sometimes darting to the front of the choir to get a closer view of the singers. The choir, made up of two rows of young girls in white blouses and below them a row of young men newly combed and suited, sat (or stood, as the occasion demanded) against the west wall of the church, facing the minister's platform at the center. Across from the choir, against the opposite wall, was a row of men with guitars. The minister, a round-faced man in his middle thirties, spoke with a wide smile into the platform microphone, announcing a song, and the church, which had been alive before in a hum of anticipation, now broke into full joy and power with the music. The six guitarists played at once, the choir sang, slightly swaying with the rhythm, and *damas* and *caballeros* alike joined in to swell and heighten the song. Women in the crowd tapped tambourines, and a small boy in the second aisle was raised on high by his mother as he shook two gourds in the happy rhythm.

When the song was over, the minister announced that there was in the audience the daughter of a Pentecostal minister in Bayamón, Puerto Rico, and that she would come to give testimony now. Below the platform microphone where the minister spoke was a microphone on the main floor, for use by those who wished to give testimony to their faith. The daughter of the minister in Bayamón came quickly forward, out of the center aisle, and stepped with determination to face squarely the microphone and the audience. She was a young and very beautiful girl, slender and straight in a plain blue dress with a slightly flared skirt. She clasped her hands behind her, and in a clear, high voice proclaimed the blessings of her faith and then asked that the audience join her in a prayer for the many people who were ill and needed help in Bayamón. She bowed her head and began to pray in the same firm, distinct voice, into the microphone. On the platform above her, the minister began to pray into his microphone — different words, but a prayer for the same purpose — and the congregation, now standing, began to speak aloud their own prayers for the people of Bayamón, the voices rising and mixing in a woven intensity of sound that was, finally, unintelligible except for its tone, which expressed its purpose, and finally lowered, ending with the minister's upraised hand and "Alleluia!"

The minister asked for other confessions of faith and a young man in a light tan suit hurried to the front, seized the microphone by the neck, and thanked God for taking him safely through the war in Korea, which he fought in after joining the U.S. Army in Puerto Rico without knowing English. The dimensions of the young man's thanks can be measured only by understanding that many Puerto Ricans were killed in Korea almost as a direct result of not knowing English, and thereby not being able to understand the commands that were given by officers who did not know Spanish to units made up almost entirely of Puerto Ricans. Slightly more than 90 per cent of the 43,434 Puerto Ricans who served in the war were volunteers. There were 3450 Puerto Rican casualties, which made one Puerto Rican casualty for every 660 residents of the island, as compared with the rate of one casualty for every 1125 residents of the U.S. mainland. Thus, the young man at the microphone had special reason for feeling, as he said, *"muy contento."*

There were many others to testify, and the thing that was common to each was the expression *"muy contento"* and the look of genuine joy on their faces. It was the look that so many people expected and missed on the faces of those who made "decisions for Christ" in the New York Billy Graham Crusade; just as the spirit of the songs and testimony of the evening had the fire and conviction that was never produced by the Reverend Dr. Graham in Madison Square Garden.

Perhaps that fire cannot be built in comfortable neighborhoods and huge arenas with rehearsed, professional programs, television shows, and promotional pamphlets. Perhaps that fire can burn only in the vacant lots of demolished hopes and the makeshift shrines that grow from the rubble of a turbulent slum. It burns in Spanish Harlem.

The spirit moves through the dark streets of need, around the white table, before the Blessed Virgin, through the pitcher of water of the dead, and into the folding chairs of the storefront parishes. Belief and despair are mixed together, producing in their vital and terrifying chemistry the necessary miracle of hope.

"*I don't dig living in Harlem — that's a long story. People here, they live in this mess and they don't have any education or any chance to get out of it. I work hard, man, eight hours a day, and I'm ashamed to tell you what I make. A guy down here, he's in it deep and he doesn't see any way out. Maybe he takes dope or alcohol, and he forgets — he wants to forget. A kid grows up here, as soon as he's old enough to go out on the street he's old enough to steal an apple. He goes from there. Maybe you go to Central Park and you see one of them kids with a bicycle and you ask him can you ride it, and he says yes and you ride it right outa the park and don't come back. You envy — you get to envy and hate.*"

꽃 꽃 꽃

Trip to the Moon

O Lord God . . . Shall thy wonders be known in the dark,
and thy righteousness in the land of forgetfulness?

— Psalm 88

Once a junkie, always a junkie.

— A neighborhood maxim
in Spanish Harlem

NORTH BROTHER ISLAND is a small patch of land just ten
minutes out in the East River by the ferry that takes you
from 134th Street. The island is in reality, if not geographically, part of the world of Spanish Harlem. It houses the
Riverside narcotics hospital for treatment of addicts under
the age of twenty-one.

New York City has a ferry ride for everyone, and even if
never taken, it is known and made a part of the life of that
particular group. Lovers in Greenwich Village read Edna St.
Vincent Millay and take the ferry to Staten Island; tourists
read "Give me your tired, your poor" and take the ferry to
the Statue of Liberty; kids in East Harlem hear the terrible
neighborhood maxim on the fate of the addict — "Once a
junkie, always a junkie" — and, in hope and desperation, take
the ferry to Riverside.

"Julio," a brown and handsome boy of seventeen who lives
on 100th Street, took it for the second time in his life after

getting an overdose of heroin. He had just served seventeen days in jail for being caught with three guys on a roof with "the works" — the syringe and needle used for injections of the drug. They had heard the cops coming and had thrown away the "stuff" — the heroin itself — but they still had the works and were sent to jail. When Julio got out he went for a fix and was given a powerful overdose that sickened him and, with the urging of friends, led him back to Riverside.

Any narcotics user in New York under the age of twenty-one may be brought to a magistrate by his family, social worker, doctor, chaplain, or similar authority, and may petition for treatment at Riverside, which is the only hospital in the world used exclusively for treating juvenile addicts, and the only community hospital (the city and state divide the annual cost of about $1,400,000) for narcotics addicts of any age in the United States. Besides the voluntary patients, boys and girls who are users may be sent by a judge on compulsory assignment after being arrested for any crime to serve part or all of their sentence under treatment at the Riverside clinic.

Julio had gone the first time on assignment from a judge after being arrested for possession of heroin, and this time applied voluntarily after coming close to death from his overdose. When some friends from the neighborhood went to visit him, he had been on the island only a week, and was still on the third floor of the main building in the detoxification ward. That is where the patients are placed at first to "kick the habit." Some, who seem completely hostile to further treatment, are sent back home after this period of physical withdrawal from the drug is completed. Others, who show a real desire for help, are sent down to the second floor, where they participate in a full program of rehabilitation that lasts six months and includes formal schooling conducted by the New York City Board of Education at the hospital's P.S. 619. The hospital usually finds that, as in most other sicknesses, the user of drugs must have a real desire to get well before he can be effectively helped. A patient who is new to narcotics and thinks he can beat the game is best released to learn through agonizing experience that he needs all the help he can get. Since Riverside began its program in 1952, there have been approximately two admissions for each patient, though some don't return at all (many pass the age limit and become ineligible) and others return several times.

Up on the third floor's detoxification ward a Negro nurse unlocked the door for Julio's visitors. Down the long corridor kids in blue pajamas and white slippers glanced up to look and then glanced away. A tall boy tapped a pair of drumsticks together, making no particular rhythm. Inside a white, sunny room off the corridor one boy sat on the floor against the wall and another sat on the edge of the bed, staring out the window. The boy on the floor was Julio. He stood up smiling when his visitors looked in the door, and invited them in. The room was barren except for beds, and the walls with their scrawled inscriptions of names and dates and a single wrinkled pin-up picture gave it the appearance of a college dorm that was vacant for the summer. The boy with the drumsticks wandered in, absently tapping at his chest, and said that Fats, an official, was coming. The other guys groaned and got up. "You can't sit down," Julio explained.

"Yeh," said the drummer, smiling at the visitors, "you gotta keep walkin' — that's therapy, man."

The Negro nurse called from outside that it was time for one of the boys to get a shot of penicillin.

"O.K., Mother —"

"We're coming, Mom."

The guys laughed, calling the lady with the needle the name they sometimes use for the pusher, who, like a mother, dispenses the good things of life.

"Mo-ther," the drummer called, smiling at the others and saying, "she really gets mad when you call her that."

Julio winced and said, "Man, she sure donno how to use that needle."

He motioned to his visitors and said, "C'mon, let's go to the solarium."

The dark hall led to a glassed-in room with a table and several scattered chairs. Scribbled on the wall in pencil was "Junkie's Place," and under it, a lopsided cross. On the section of wall that ran up the center of the mural made by the arc of windows, someone had drawn a coat of arms consisting of the works — needle, syringe, and belt on a field of chipping green plaster, set against the wide and sunswept view of the New York City skyline.

Julio perched on the table and asked about things in the neighborhood and what had happened to "Joey," one of the guys who was caught with him up on the roof. Dick, who had come from the neighborhood, said that Joey was still in jail.

"Man, I was lucky," Julio said. "I took the rap and I thought they'd keep me up a long time. When the judge cut me loose I was real surprised. He asked how long I'd been in and they said seventeen days and he said 'Time served.' I'd already kicked my habit then — in jail, cold turkey, but it wasn't too bad. Another guy there he tried to hang himself — used his belt, but when he got up there and kicked away the stool he started screamin' and the hack came and took him down. Me, I did it all under the covers — sweating, vomitin', all of it. Then in about four days I was up and started working out. I was O.K., except before I went in some cop beat me up for talking — down in the bullpen — and I was in handcuffs."

Julio rubbed his cheek and stared out the window, shaking his head.

"All for a lousy cigarette," he said. "That's what it was I was trying to get."

Dick asked how he had gotten his overdose after he got out of jail. Julio said he had met one of the guys who claimed he had some "pure" heroin.

"He said he had a habit on this pure stuff and I could have some but I better not have much. I thought he was just talkin', and I said if he could take it pure I could too, but I guess it was real strong stuff and I got an O.D. I guess he really had a habit with this pure stuff. I'd only been out of jail a few days when it happened, and then I came over here. Listen, if you see my sister — Anna, the little one — tell her to tell my mother where I am. O.K.?"

Dick said he would, and that he'd tell everyone that Julio was in good shape. Julio said it was true, and all he wanted now was to leave the hospital. There was nothing to do on the third floor and all this waiting — nothing had happened except that he had been in a fight with a Negro.

"There's lots of colored guys here," he said. "They think they run the island. We call 'em Cocolos. It's some Spanish name for coconut — like coconut head. We tell 'em this is their home — we say, 'Man, you never had it so good — you never had food so good; outside you got no home. Here's your home.' They try to bully you around, take your commissary stuff — candy and cigarettes. You got to prove yourself. They tried to take mine when I first was here so I put on the gloves with one of their guys and now they leave me alone."

Julio smiled and patted the taut flesh of his stomach. His body was the well-proportioned shape and rich brown color whose achievement is the goal of country club lifeguards.

"I used to work out a lot," he said. "I worked on the bar bells and boxing. People were surprised when I got hooked, I guess."

He was quiet for a moment, rubbing his stomach.

"It started one night up at the Palladium, my girl left with another guy. I was mad, real mad, and a guy offered me a snort. I took it O.K., and liked it. I took some more, and then I started skin-poppin' and then that wasn't doing me any good and I had to get on the main-line. It didn't really take me long to get hooked. I remember one night I was lying in bed trying not to think about it and I couldn't think of anything else and I got dressed and ran out into the street, lookin' for a fix — and I knew I was hooked. I was getting it about three times a day and chipping in with another guy to buy the stuff. It was costing me $15 a day. I hocked a lot of my clothes and then I stole my little sister's watch and my brother-in-law's camera and my big sister's radio. My big sister and brother-in-law, they don't want to have anything to do with me any more. But I'll make it up to 'em when I get out. I'm gonna get me a job — get my clothes outa the pawnshop. I wanna get back and get me some nice clothes and a girl — that's the only way."

Julio shook his head and said, "I won't get hooked again —

this is the second time and now I don't want to mess around with the stuff any more. If I do, I don't want to come back here. I don't dig this place any more — it's getting too strict. If you go downstairs to the second floor they want to keep you six months now. That's too long. You come in voluntary, they oughta let you out when you want to. Last year I was in for fifty-two days — twice I tried to swim out — once I got busted in the river and once on the grounds, just as I was about to dive. Now, they want me to stay the six months — get helped they say. I haven't got any habit now, but they don't know it. The other day this new Doc they got came around, and I told him I had a habit and he gave me medication — man, but I got high that night! These Docs don't know nothin'. I called my social worker today and told him to get me outa here. I don't know when I'm gonna get out. My psychiatrist says I need therapy. I wanna get out — I'm through with stuff. And man, when I get out I'm staying out. I'm never comin' back here again. If I do get hooked again, man, I'm not comin' here — I'm gonna get an O.D."

Julio put his hands on his knees and nodded his head toward the floor; emphatically, as if he had just discovered a truth.

"That's the only way out for a junkie."

He sat for a while without speaking and then raised his head, a broad white smile across the darkness of his face. Nothing was left to say.

From the bright, clean silence of the Riverside solarium it seemed a long way to the violent streets where Julio came from and where he would soon return to work out his fate. But it is only that ten-minute ferry ride, five minutes more on the subway, a few minutes' walk, and then you are "home" — and not a solarium as far as the eye can see. On East 100th

Street a block from the river the dark-faced buildings hem you in, and the free majestic arc of the Triborough Bridge seems only a cardboard backdrop hung in the distance. The cars speed one-way north along First Avenue, seldom stopping, as if on a track that has no relation to the neighborhood it happens to pass through. The life moving past and the life in the distance has no reality, except as it represents the hope of escape, which is cheap and is shared by so many people — especially the young ones — who live in the slums of Spanish Harlem. The old ones more often are resigned to this world, and it seems too late to think of something else.

Some people want to go back to San Juan, or the green, interior hills of Puerto Rico. Some want to go to the Bronx. "Manny," a young father who was graduated from the neighborhood school system without knowing how to read or write, is studying at night to make up the years of his loss and someday "take up agriculture," which is just about as far as you can get from these streets. "Frankie," a sixteen-year-old narcotics addict, told some friends that he wanted to go to the Dominican Republic where he has relatives who work in an office —"not just work but run that office." Several weeks after this declaration he was seen on the block with his eyes large and glassy, his body twitching, and a friend yelled, "Hey man, you look strung out again," to which he jerked a nod and did not say anything about the Dominican Republic.

The dream of escape is a dream of the young, and the addicts, not only in this neighborhood but everywhere, are mostly young people. The Federal Bureau of Narcotics has estimated that of the 17,563 known addicts (inevitably short of the actual total) in New York and northern New Jersey, more than 2000 are under 21; more than 10,000 are under

30; only 1737 are over 40. That is no country for old men.

Yet officials often squint from the facts. William Jansen, superintendent of the New York City public schools, testified before the State Joint Legislative Committee on Narcotics Study in 1958 that for the period March 1956 to April 1957 there was a total of 16 known drug users in the city school system — an encouraging drop from the 173 known users reported in 1951. This statistic is based on the assumption that schoolteachers know how many students in their classes are using drugs. After the figure appeared in the press, the Reverend Norman Eddy walked over to the candy store on 100th Street and asked some kids he knew were users if they were a part of this statistic. They said they hadn't been counted. During the six-month period from January 1, 1957, to September 1, 1957, a total of 16 juvenile addicts from the neighborhood who were known to the East Harlem Protestant Parish went to the Riverside hospital for treatment. The school board total for the whole city could be gathered in a single neighborhood. The optimistic total of 16 users evidently also excluded the more than 150 students of P.S. 169 at North Brother Island.

In revealing the great "decline" in student users, the school board felt that perhaps it was partially due to the fact that instruction about narcotics and its dangers had been made a part of regular health courses in 1952. There is no way to estimate just how much the pupils have learned about drugs from their teachers, but it can be known what the students knew before — and the knowledge was not from books. In 1951 a ninth grade teacher in Spanish Harlem asked her class to write a paper on "What I Know about Narcotics." The answers perhaps give a better picture than any statistics about the reality of students and drugs in this neighborhood. The pupils instructed the teacher with information such as this:

One day me and my friends were playing baseball in a lot, and this car pulled up and one of the men called over and asked us would we like to buy some stuff that will make us drunk and feel good for the rest of the day. He said we'll be able to play ball much better and I said no because I knew what he was talking about. In the summer early in the morning around Fifth Avenue and 110th Street a car comes by and men line up to get this injection, but when the car does not come by, the men almost go crazy.

A lot of boys on my block uses it. The kind they use comes in a little container which they call a cap. The name that they call it by is Horse [heroin]. Some of them puts it on a piece of a match box cover and inhale it. But some of the boys says afterwards it makes you scratch a lot. They won't tell where they get it from but they say it cost $1.00 for a cap. A cap is red with a white band in the middle of it . . . it also makes the boys throw up. You can tell when someone has been using it by looking at his eyes. He also scratches a lot.

I saw some men in a hallway one day as I was coming from school. They had a long white stick, some people call it reefers. Some call it marijuana. It had an awful smell. They would take a little puff, then smoke a cigarette behind it to make the smell go away. That was suppose to make them high. Another kind of narcotics is a cap of horse, which costs at least a dollar. The way they take it to get high is to put a little tiny batch in the top of the cap and sniff it. It doesn't have very much of a smell. Another way to take Horse is pour all the powder out on a flat mirror and take a straw and you sniff it with the straw into your nose.

I see nothing, hear nothing, say nothing, know nothing.

The last author had grown much older than his friends. He knew too much already — what is there to say to the agents of the outside world? The escape through heroin sets you apart from that world forever.

The trip is expensive — profoundly more before it is over than the going rate of $7 for a single heroin "fix" (injection with a needle). But that small initial investment will take you farther away for the money than any other ticket of transportation. It is not, however, a round-trip ticket. In medical terminology there is no such thing as a "cured" addict; there are only "arrested" addicts — but the traveler who wants to get out right away has no room to bargain. The pusher can wait, business is good, and if he waits long enough the moment may come when he can get you too, no questions asked, just the "stuff" that will take you away.

The pushers are liberals, possessing no sense of discrimination, and the "junk" they sell was one of the few things offered with no questions asked to the Puerto Rican migrants who settled in Harlem. The junk itself knows no distinctions of race, creed, or color. Negroes, Italians, and Irishmen living in the neighborhood before and along with the Puerto Ricans — ministers in small southern towns, respectable doctors in large cities, men and women, boys and girls — all have been able to enter the mysteries, delights, terrors, and destructions of the habit in this nation which has a larger number of narcotics addicts than all the other countries of the Western world combined.

But the experience is different for the people who live in slums, like Spanish Harlem. It is not a physiological difference, for the famous actor with a fantastic income undergoes the same convulsions of need, once addicted, as the penniless father of a family on relief. The difference is that the man with money can easily keep his need supplied. The man with no money must get it; his body demands the drug, and the drug, because of the illegality of its sales and purchase, has become outrageously expensive. An ounce of heroin costs $5 in Lebanon. By the time it is smuggled inside the United States it is worth $8750. One $7 fix usually contains three or four grains of heroin. Sometimes the "stuff" is weak, and contains only two grains, which means that the user may not be satisfied and must pay another $7 for another fix. It costs at least $50 a week to maintain a habit, and becomes progressively more expensive as the habit gets worse. The wealthy man or the doctor who is an addict merely pays or takes from his own supply and concentrates his worries and fears on the habit itself. The man so poor that he has to live in the slums must obviously face the question of where to get all that money. There are only two answers, and both are a crime. One is to steal. The other is to become a pusher, and earn the junk you need by dispensing junk to others.

This type of neighborhood or smalltime pusher who is also a junkie himself does not get rich from the fabulous profits of the traffic in stuff. He makes only enough to keep him in his habit, which keeps him at his job of pushing — and yet he runs a daily risk with the same high penalties of punishment as the wealthy, unseen directors of the traffic, who almost literally never get caught. The law makes no distinction between the pusher who is an addict himself and a victim of the system he works for, and the pusher who is in the business for profit and out of his own free will.

"Boppo Cruz" is a neighborhood pusher out of East Harlem, who has served several terms in the penitentiary and always returns to his profession — the only one he knows — as inevitably as he returns to his habit when he gets back home. He first was hooked at the age of sixteen, became a pusher several years after, and now at twenty-seven is a master of the intricate skills of the trade and possessor of a habit commensurate with his own great power to supply it.

One night Boppo dropped by a friend's house for dinner — but now, already, the words and phrases that describe the course of affairs in the ordinary world become inadequate and badly out of focus when applied to the world of the addict. Boppo does not drop by a friend's house. Nothing he does, no movement he makes, can be reported with any such casual terminology. Boppo was high, and he entered like a man who is entering a room full of helium gas. He seemed to be floating — and yet, there was nothing restful in it, for the movements of his body never stopped, never relaxed. When he reached for a cup of coffee, when he transferred a piece of cake from its plate to his own plate, it seemed that he would miss — drop the cup, drop the cake, and yet he never did. He seemed to be moving in a shadow world, in which his body was the only thing of substance, and everything else — the other people, the furniture, the cups, the cake — were only shadow and didn't have substance until he touched them, grasped them. Up to the very moment of contact with any object it seemed that he expected his hand to move right through it as a hand moves through a ray of light.

Boppo was sharply dressed in slacks, sport coat, a plaid Ivy League button-down shirt, and a leather cap. He jerked away from the table when he finished eating, stood up, pulled a roll of bills about three inches thick from his hip pocket and held them before his friend.

"Hey, you see, I'm doing all right in the narcotics field. Like sixty bucks a day now."

The friend said he hadn't seen Boppo around the neighborhood lately, and wondered where he was doing business.

"I'm working the West Side," Boppo said. "It's good, but it's rough. There's a lotta stoolpigeons over there. You gotta be careful."

Boppo shoved the wad of bills back into his pocket, yanked out the chair, sat again.

"You know, somebody oughta do something about these kids around here. This block. 'Tony' just got out of Riverside, and I could hook him any time."

Boppo snapped his fingers — "Like that."

"You see him, tell him to stay away from me. All I gotta do is go up and say 'Hey, man, how about a little fix? It won't take much to get high.' And he'd go — him with a wife and kids."

Boppo slammed his fist on the table.

"Weak bastard!"

He reached for what was left of his cup of coffee — swigged the end of it, set it down.

"Why does a guy like him look up to me?"

"Because you're older," Boppo's friend said. "And powerful. Power with words. Power with people. Powerful personality. Power to hurt people."

Boppo was silent a moment.

"Yeh? Well, why do most people look down on me?"

"Because you're a junkie."

Boppo jerked up again to a stand. "I'm no goddamned junkie. I'm a Drug Addict. You know that. A goddamned junkie steals from his folks, donno what it's all about. I'm through with all that. I'm a Drug Addict."

"Sure, but a lot of people don't know the difference."

Boppo — quiet — "Yeh, you're right."

Boppo's friend mentioned something about responsibility to guys who looked up to him. Boppo, moving around the kitchen now, facing off from each wall and turning to another as if his body were reacting, being pushed away by the solid surfaces, a bull in a pen, spoke, deeply: " 'No man is an island entire of itself; every man is a piece of the continent, a part of the main . . . any man's death diminishes me, because I am involved in mankind. And therefore never send to know for whom the bell tolls; it tolls for thee . . .' " He paused. Then in his ordinary voice: "John Donne. I know that crap."

Moving toward the front room now, his friend getting up to follow, Boppo stopped before leaving, turned, spoke in farewell: "If you hear of anything to do to make a living besides narcotics that isn't dull, let me know."

And Boppo was gone.

His friend has no idea when Boppo will be back, or when he again will be caught and sent to jail. The question is not so much *if* as *when*, for the neighborhood pusher. Above him in the hierarchy, the middleman or peddler runs much less of a risk and makes a great deal more money. He goes on daily rounds to make distributions to the neighborhood pushers but never administers a fix himself and does not come into contact with the customers.

New York being the most democratic city in the world, it is possible for the people of the Puerto Rican minority group to rise to a position of profit from the illegal traffic in drugs that preys upon their fellow migrants. Many of the middlemen or peddlers in Spanish Harlem are Puerto Ricans. Some of them make as much as a thousand dollars a week. And yet, in the end, the "stuff" is always a cheat — except to the invisible men at the top who reap the big-time profits. The peddlers can't let their profits show, except to their colleagues. They usually gather at a certain bar (for a while it was one on the corner of 111th Street and Madison), though it necessarily changes from time to time as the word gets widely spread that this is where they can be found.

The peddlers' gatherings provide some of the few occasions when they are able to appreciate each others' hidden wealth, which, if exposed too brazenly, could lead to the secret of its illegal accumulation. None have the lavish homes their money could buy. None have cars. They travel by taxi, a professional transit that leaves no record of expense. A great amount of their money goes into gambling, which gives prestige to the man who can afford to lose so much and also helps him dispose of the money whose use is so limited. The peddlers often plan great sorties to night clubs and high-priced parties, drinking the best, and dropping hundreds of dollars in the desperate effort to wring some reward from the riches that, finally, mock their existence.

Such are the ways of education offered to Puerto Rican migrants by New York City. And, different from foreign immigrants or other minority migrants within the U.S. mainland, the Puerto Ricans who become addicted to drugs are sometimes returned with their burdens to the land they came from. Puerto Ricans have come to Harlem, as well as other parts of New York, learned about dope, and then, their lessons completed, have often been sent back to Puerto Rico by the courts that arrested them. A lawyer representing an addict may make several suggestions for "rehabilitation" that will affect his client's sentence — perhaps eliminate it — and one of the methods of getting people of Puerto Rican birth or parentage off the rap is to promise their return to Puerto Rico. It is not of course a practice for addicts from Texas arrested in New York City to get off the rap by having their lawyer promise the client's return to Texas.

Yet this is the sort of thing the government accepts as a kind of packaged "solution" and punishment for the Puerto Rican addict. It lives within the myth of minority prejudice, along with the notion that dark-skinned people are somehow depraved and born to be affected by the illegal ecstasies of drugs. Those who are born in Spanish Harlem often are — though it is due to the site, and not the source of their birth.

Psychologists looking for solutions have discovered this again and again. Dr. Isidor Chein, Professor of Psychology at New York University, conducted a study of juvenile narcotics use in New York City in 1955 and found that three fourths of the adolescent users lived in just 15 per cent of the city's census tracts; that these tracts constituted the poorest, most crowded, and most physically dilapidated areas of the city; that within these tracts the drug use was highest where education and income were lowest and there existed the most serious breakdown of family relationships; that these areas were in the large part centers of Negro and Puerto Rican population; and that, also, Negro and Puerto Rican residential areas that were less acute in their social and economic problems had low rates of drug use.

Despite its publicity the problem of narcotics addiction and its treatment is nearly as perplexing to professionals as it was twenty years ago; doctors, psychologists, social workers, and ministers search for the answers. The people search too, their material being not graphs and statistics but the faces of neighbors and family and friends. On Broadway and Long Island "dope" means a book or a movie; in Spanish Harlem it means a face. The geography of knowledge is sharp and distinct. From 50th Street to 96th on Park Avenue, "narcotics" is Nelson Algren or Frank Sinatra in *The Man with the Golden Arm;* north of 96th Street, it is Tony, who was on the block all morning, high, or Joe, who just got back from the hospital at Lexington.

Louis León, known as Pee-Wee, had seen it all happen again and again, and wondered if there wasn't some answer for the neighborhood. Pee-Wee is a man of broad girth and broad shoulders, and on them he carries, more than most men, the troubles of his fellows. His sometimes tough and challenging exterior, barbed with the rough and painfully honest phraseology of the neighborhood, hides a deep perception of other peoples' problems and a deep concern for them. Pee-Wee is only twenty-one years old but that fact, too, is hidden by the age and experience of his heavy, shadowed face.

Pee-Wee is one of the lucky ones — and strong ones — who were able to grow up on one of the hottest blocks of narcotics traffic in the world without getting hooked. He did, however, have his brush with one form of narcotics that was at the time inevitable. He learned about "snorting" (inhaling cocaine) in high school. It was extracurricular and required.

"If I wanted to live," he once recalled, "I had to get on it. Everybody was on it, so for six months I did and was miserable. I was lucky. There were thirty-six guys in my high school class. I've lost track of some, but today there are only three I know of out doing something — me, one guy who's an air force pilot, and one who's an engineer. The rest I know of are scattered in and out of jails and hospitals from here to Lexington."

Cocaine is not a physically addicting drug, but most of the guys who went through its use moved on to heroin, which like morphine becomes almost as necessary for the body of the addict as water for the body of the ordinary person. Since cocaine and marijuana, which is the most widely used narcotic among adolescents in the neighborhood, are not addicting, many kids believe they can cope with heroin too, and move on to it as the source of a bigger kick and, sometimes, proof of being a man.

They of course end up as less than men — creatures dependent on jails and hospitals and the harmless-looking white powder known as heroin. Pee-Wee saw his friends and neighbors thus transformed to a life of terror and tragedy, and in his own way tried to help. He learned the junkies' scuttlebutt and tried to be their friend. He started advising them to apply for admission to the federal narcotics hospital at Lexington, Kentucky, where they could kick it with medical help and follow-up rehabilitation program that gave them a better chance when they got back home.

But Lexington is far from New York (although closer than the only other federal narcotics hospital in Fort Worth, Texas) and the trip with a stay of at least four months and sometimes six was hard for the neighborhood guys to accept. As Pee-Wee pointed out to them, though, and as their own experience often taught them, it was better than going to a local jail and being confined for thirty days to kick "cold turkey," which is without benefit of medication and guarantees a physiological experience of extreme and extended agony. Some who try it "cold turkey" on the outside attempt

— and sometimes succeed — committing suicide before getting through it.

Pee-Wee's advice to addicts was, necessarily, hopelessly limited by the laws and facilities of the state and nation. For addicts in New York under twenty-one years of age, there is Riverside. For addicts over that age there is almost nothing. Under the existing laws, no narcotics addict may be referred to any public hospital in New York City. This often means that an addict suffering from another illness may not be able to enter a hospital for treatment because he also suffers from the illness of drug addiction. A pregnant mother who is also an addict will not ordinarily be accepted by a New York City hospital for delivery of her baby. An exception was made once in 1957 when a pregnant woman from East Harlem who was addicted to heroin was admitted to a hospital in the Bronx under heavy pressure from church and social agencies, but the doctors later said that they did not want to make such practice a rule. The only facilities in New York City for adult narcotics addicts are maintained not by the Department of Health but the Department of Correction. The man or woman who is suffering the pains and tortures of the drug disease is sent not to a hospital but to a jail. An adult addict may apply to the Department of Correction and be sent to the jail at Rikers Island or the Women's House of Detention. Commissioner Anna Kross of the City Department of Correction testified before the State of New York Joint Legislative Committee on Narcotics about the treatment offered for addicts at Rikers Island and the Women's House of Detention, and summed it up in a single word: "Nothing."

Out of the frustration of this kind of answer for addicts,

Pee-Wee went to Norman Eddy in the fall of 1956 and asked if the East Harlem Protestant Parish couldn't "do something." Norm knew many addicts himself, and had also met the dead-end frustration of trying to point them toward any answers. He was ready to try the mysterious something — anything — to help.

Out of their desire and the neighborhood's need was born the Narcotics Committee of the East Harlem Protestant Parish. It offers not salvation but hope and understanding and a constant effort to find solutions. The people in East Harlem have a reasonable lack of respect for committees (there have been so many, and with so little effect), but this one was different. Committees are not ordinarily formed to deal with the deepest and most unmentionable problems of the neighborhood. When the committee first was formed, addicts and friends of addicts were reluctant to come to a public discussion because of the shame of their problem. The growing attendance of the weekly meetings is the sign of the changing attitudes toward addiction as a sickness instead of a crime that the committee is helping to bring about. Talk that was once known only behind closed doors was brought out into the open, and people of the neighborhood began to argue the theories they so long had kept to themselves. Pee-Wee once got into a debate after one of the meetings with María Flores, who had also seen close friends become trapped by the drug and had come to the work of the committee in the same spirit of hope and desire to help as Pee-Wee had.

Pee-Wee was saying, "I don't think they start because of conditions or the way the neighborhood is. They start because it's a kick. They start out blowing pot, thinking that's all right, and then that's not enough and they take a snort and then they're skin-poppin' and then before they know it they're on the main-line."

Those are the degrees of education: "blowing pot," which is smoking marijuana; "snorting," or inhaling cocaine, neither of which are addicting but commonly lead to "skin-popping," insertion in the body of a needle containing heroin, and finally, "main-lining," which means insertion of the needle with heroin into a large vein in the arm, and thus directly into the bloodstream.

María listened carefully to Pee-Wee's explanation that the kids progressed through these stages purely for kicks and then shook her head.

"Pee-Wee, I say they get on it because of these miserable conditions here. They do it for that, and for family problems. Some of these kids don't have any home. Some of them that do are all upset. Sometimes it's psychological. Some of these kids that get hooked, they do it for punishment."

Pee-Wee smiled and said, "Listen — when you're flyin' through the air at ninety miles an hour and grabbin' hunks of cheese off the moon, that's no punishment."

But the trip to the moon must end, and the traveler must sink from being high to being home again, and home is Spanish Harlem — the block and the tenement, the gang and the family that perhaps is no family at all but a young deserted mother like Providencia and her seven kids, held together by hope and a relief check for $105 every two weeks, out of which has to come food and clothes and rent for eight people, and sometimes a fix for the oldest son. Home is where it all began, and back from the moon it is now even worse because the traveler is sick and everyone knows where he's been and only his friends who have habits are still his friends. The guys who are off it are afraid to go around with him because, if they do, they too will be typed as junkies.

Pee-Wee and María and Norm Eddy and the committee that has grown from their concern have provided the first opportunity for the addicts to have a place to go in public where they are accepted with all their burdens, and friends who are not addicted who are willing to be seen with them, talk with them, try to help them get a job and, when it's needed, help them get the money for the trip to Lexington.

The barren back room of the Family Center of the Parish on East 100th Street serves as a meeting place for the committee. Folding chairs and benches are formed in a circle beneath the fluorescent lights still wound with red and green and yellow crepe paper used for decoration at the kids' canteen dances Friday nights. The first hour is only for addicts and their families. They talk with a psychologist from the prison hospital at Hart's Island who has volunteered to come every week for a nominal fee and conduct a session of group therapy. Also present is Ramón Muñoz, the committee chairman whose free time and energy are all devoted to the cause. Ramón is a veteran himself of Lexington, and one of the few who have found a lasting cure from the habit. Mostly parents come to this session and are schooled in the grim education their children have undergone. Sometimes addicts come, wanting help and advice. Often they come to get the application papers for Lexington.

One night a short fellow with a broad, bronze face came in and took a chair on the outer edge of the circle. His black hair was combed carefully high, and his blue sport shirt hung out evenly over newly pressed brown slacks. He spoke quickly in an anxious English that attempted to cover its errors with its speed.

"I wanta go K.Y.," he said.

He had heard about the Narcotics Committee and heard that one of the ministers could get him the papers for application to the federal hospital at Lexington, Kentucky. Ramón Muñoz explained that the man for that was Norm Eddy, who was on vacation, but that his replacement should be around in about an hour.

"Well," the stranger said, "I wait. I wanta kick it. I don't have a bad habit. I only got a six months habit now. I gonna kick it for good before it gets any worse."

A psychologist who was there that night from Rikers Island spoke across the room to explain that even if he got the papers sent right away it took at least several weeks to get accepted, and it might be wise to make plans until then.

"Sure," said Ramón. "You can go out and get yourself committed to Rikers Island for thirty days, and then go straight from there to Kentucky."

The stranger squinted unpleasantly.

"Yeh," he said, "but they fingerprint you out there, and then you got a record."

Ramón said no, that it didn't give you a record.

"How are you going to do it otherwise?" the psychologist asked. "How are you going to stay off the stuff until you get to Lexington?"

"Man, I wanta kick it, that's all. When I want to I want to."

"Sure, but your body says something different," Ramón said. He raised his hands toward his chest, his fingers clawlike pointing to himself.

"Your nerves, your body, it gets you." He lowered his hands to relax on his legs again, and his dark face half-cocked to the stranger was eloquent.

"You got to have help," he said. "You think you have will power but you got to have help too."

The stranger jerked his head to each side of the room.

"Nobody kicks it by himself?"

Another newcomer had quietly slipped in and sat down on a chair away from the questioning stranger. He was a tall stringy man with a sallow, pinched face. His voice was high and thin as he said, "I kick it myself in Philadelphia."

The bronze-faced man turned to him anxiously.

"Yeh?"

"Three or four years ago, I kick it down there, staying with these friends I have."

"Yeh! Out of town. I thought myself maybe I go up-state, up to some farm or job in some town, upstate. Out of the city."

"You know anyone upstate?" the psychologist asked.

The stranger hesitated, and shook his head.

"You can't just go up someplace by yourself, " the psychologist said. "You've got to have some friends to stay with who can help you if you want to do it like that."

"Look," Ramón said, "I don't want you to think we are pressing you or anything to go to Rikers Island, but if you want to yourself, maybe it's the best thing. You get help, you're with people to help you, then you get out and go to Kentucky."

"Yeh, well, maybe so."

"And what will happen if you just hang around?" the psychologist asked. "You're going to need the stuff, and you're

out of a job now and don't have money. Where are you going to get the money if you need the stuff bad — if you're
sick? You're going to do something to get it, and then maybe
be in real trouble."

"Yeh," the fellow said emphatically. "Yeh, you right. You
right. I better to go to Rikers maybe. I'm going to kick,
otherwise I don't come here in the first place. Maybe I go to
Rikers first."

Everyone agreed it was the best course to take, and the
second newcomer began telling about how he kicked it with
these friends of his in Philadelphia and never went back on it.
The bronze-faced stranger got up and lit a cigarette. After a
while, he asked when the man would be there who could get
him the papers for Kentucky. Ramón said it ought to be
pretty soon. A few more people came in, and the stranger lit
another cigarette and went to stand at the door.

About half an hour later, fourteen or fifteen people were
there and Ramón began the open meeting, as usual with "The
Serenity Prayer": "God, give us the courage to accept the
things we can't change, to change the things we can, and the
wisdom to know the difference."

The several subcommittees gave their reports, and after a
while Ramón mentioned to the young minister who was there
as Norm Eddy's replacement that a fellow was there wanting
papers for Lexington.

Ramón looked around the room, but the stranger was gone.

"He was here earlier," Ramón said. "Maybe he'll be back."

The meeting went on, and closed with its prayer, and the
coffee was served, and the people talked; and the stranger who
was going to kick it was never seen again.

The weekly meetings are a grim education for the outsiders.

The second hour of the meeting is open to anyone who is interested, and mainly they try to learn about the problem. From ten or fifteen to as many as fifty people show up to hear guest speakers talk about narcotics, and have their theories challenged by the people at the meeting who often know of cases that don't fit the visitors' theories. Psychologists, doctors, professors, musicians, policemen, detectives, and social workers have come and talked to the group and listened to them. It sometimes happens that in this dusty room the forces that move one another but never meet come face to face. The shock of recognition is often great. One night an official from the prison hospital at Rikers Island came, and was asked by one of the boys who had been there why the addicts were put to work at hard labor four or five days after they entered, sometimes when they were still sick from the process of withdrawal. The Rikers official explained that "many of you fellows come back again and again — sometimes two and three times a year. Well, we instituted that hard labor so you wouldn't get the idea we were running a country club out there."

The audience broke into loud, long laughter.

In the end, it is usually the audience that supplies the most enlightenment. One night a discussion got going about how people who had never known the drug could help and be friends with the guys who were getting out of hospitals. Some guys who had made that trip were saying it was one of the hardest things of all, and yet it was not altogether the fault of the folks at home.

"It's not just society that can't accept you," one boy who was back from Riverside said. "It's you can't accept society, too. Once you've used narcotics you band together with other guys who have — like everybody else seems square, you know? I feel the problem is adjusting to the others, who all seem square — then you've got it made."

The addict stands outside the square world that has never known the needle and can never understand, and its rules and formulas, its very words, can often no longer touch him. He makes his own, and in the dark hours of his personal terror he finds that even their prayers no longer have meaning. A young man who lives on 100th Street wrote this psalm for himself:

Heroin is my shepherd; I shall always want.
It maketh me to lie down in gutters;
It leadeth me beside still madness.
It destroyeth my soul.
It leadeth me in the paths of hell for its name's sake.
Yea, though I walk through the valley of the shadow of death,
I will fear no evil; for Heroin art with me;
My syringe and spike will comfort me.
Thou puttest me to shame in the presence of mine enemies.
Thou anointest my head with madness; my cup runneth over
*   with sorrow.*
Surely hate and evil shall follow me all the days of my life,
And I will dwell in the house of misery and disgrace forever.

On rooftops and tenements and hallways stinking with garbage, from vacant lots glittering with broken glass and streets alive with children and music, comes the unspoken "Amen" of those who know.

A fifteen-year-old guy had gone to the dance and pulled out a gun and started shooting into the crowd. Four people were wounded and the cops came and rounded up all the guys and took them to the Precinct headquarters on 104th Street. The guys were all lined up outside and Diega, who was always half drunk and cursed the kids except when they got into trouble, came running to them and stretched her arms to embrace as many as possible and said to the cops, "They are all my sons."

Conservatives without a Cause

> . . . and the boys lay inert on the cross of a yawn
> and stretched muscle.
>
> — "The King of Harlem,"
>   FEDERICO GARCÍA LORCA

BETWEEN a plumbing and heating supply store and the Veteran Bar and Grill on upper First Avenue is a boarded storefront painted black and covered with silver prints of hands. There is no other mark of identification, unless the door swings open and the sign that says "Members Only" stares with its high silver letters at the street. Any passer-by from the neighborhood knows that the sign, though not inviting, is at least not menacing. This is the clubhouse, the home, and the hope, of a teen-age gang that has given up fighting and "gone social" in a world of poverty and violence. They call themselves The Conservatives.

In another neighborhood, The Conservatives might be the name of a political club. It would never be the name of a political club in the precincts that cover the east side of Harlem. This is not because the area is totally barren of Republicans; but rather because its citizens seem to have some instinctive knowledge that gives everything its proper name in the most profound sense. The names of political clubs are names like Caribe Club and Miami Club — names that have no relation to the neighborhood except by a large extension of imagination; names that are not about the place itself, and are therefore appropriate to its politics.

The name of a teen-age gang that gives up fighting is of course The Conservatives; that is what the issue is about. It is about preservation of life in a neighborhood that has a tradition of violence. The tradition began when the neighborhood began to crumble and became a home for the poor; it has been passed on from strangers who speak Russian and strangers who speak Italian to strangers who speak Spanish, from generation to generation. The gangs are only a part of that larger violence that lives where men are hungry and angry, and neighbors look upon people of a different color or language as enemy invaders; where the bodies of junkies cry for a fix that only money can buy, and the cops are seen as colonial troops of an unsympathetic government.

The cops in this neighborhood are not looked upon by its people as protectors of life to whom you run in time of trouble. Rather they are the enemies you run away from — and even that is dangerous. More than once a kid who was yelled at to halt by a cop has been shot down when he didn't stop. The largest funeral held in East Harlem, besides the funeral of Congressman Vito Marcantonio, was the funeral of Georgie Martínez, a sixteen-year-old boy who was shot and killed by Detective Philip Dennehy on September 15, 1955, while being pursued as a rape suspect. Suspect Martínez failed to stop when Dennehy yelled for him to halt. Dennehy shot, and it was proved later that Georgie Martínez was innocent of the suspected charge. His reputation was restored but his life was not.

In 1949 Patrolman Samuel Rubenfeld shot and killed a

twenty-year-old boy named Herminión Miranda who also failed to halt when ordered. Miranda had been in a dice game on the street and, according to police reports, had handed a pistol to a friend after it was over. According to ministers who gathered from churches of all faiths throughout East Harlem to lead a black-robed protest parade in front of the 23rd Precinct station on East 104th Street, Miranda ran because he refused to give a $2 bribe to Rubenfeld to release him.

On January 4, 1956, a boy was killed at 101st Street and First Avenue. The Christian Action Committee of the East Harlem Protestant Parish reported on January 12, 1956, that as a result of that death, between thirty and forty young boys from the neighborhood were rounded up by the police, taken to the 23rd Precinct station, and beaten and tortured in attempts to get confessions.

It was after this last incident, which involved many boys who were members or friends of the Parish, that its ministers asked for and got a meeting with Mayor Wagner on January 18, 1956, to discuss police brutality in the neighborhood. Norman Eddy said at the meeting that the Mayor perhaps did not fully realize the bitterness that the people in East Harlem, from grandmothers to young children, feel toward the police. The Mayor asked why they felt this bitterness. Norman Eddy cited the case of Georgie Martínez and others like it, and the last incident in which so many of the kids had been beaten up at the precinct station. He introduced a boy named Papo DeLeon, who told how he had been beaten up in that questioning.

The Mayor was very sorry to hear these things, and he promised improvement. He told the group from East Harlem that the Police Academy had recently instituted a course in conjunction with the City College of New York that would emphasize "the human factor" in police training. As in so many of the instances when the people of the city's worst slum meet face to face with the city's governing officials, the distance seems too great to bridge. The Mayor speaks of courses in human relations; in the neighborhood of the 23rd Precinct, adolescent boys speak of two detectives known locally as Mutt and Jeff who have a reputation for especially expert methods of brutality.

After the Mayor's meeting, Police Department representatives came to the neighborhood to hold discussions, which they hoped would improve relations between the police and the people. In one of those meetings the kids were complaining about the rough treatment the cops always gave them, and one of the Police representatives said that after all, the police had to maintain discipline and a little discipline was good for the boys. He cited how hard the discipline is at West Point, and what fine fellows it turns out. One of the boys with a small imagination pointed out that this was East Harlem — not West Point.

Despite the many nods toward community protests, action and attitudes do not seem to have greatly altered. A young man who was picked up later in that same year for questioning on a murder charge explained his experience this way:

"I was working with the Sanitation Department at the time, and somebody came along with a cop and said, 'That's him,' and they took me in. They tried to get me to sign a confession. They hit me with the sticks, you know, till after a while I swear I began to wonder myself whether I really did it. Finally they got my boss down and he swore I was working during the time it happened and that was the end of it. Except they kept my boss a long time to question him, and when I got out I lost my job."

In time of terror a citizen of East Harlem thinks twice before calling the police. And yet there are many times when police are needed. The strains and tensions of a neighborhood constantly changing in population, with new groups and old groups of different races and nationalities looking toward one another in fear, are powerful and always present. They are sometimes crystallized in scenes of violence and anguish, like one that took place late one night in July of 1957, on First Avenue and 102nd Street.

A bearded bum lay asleep in an open truck, and two men passed, looked in, and walked a short way down the block. They stopped, looked back, and one lit a cigarette and moved back into the shadows of the tenements, watching both ways. The other, shorter man had returned to the truck. He jerked open the door, jerked out the bum, and dragged him quickly up across the sidewalk onto the doorsteps of a building, propped him against its wall, and hit him in the face very rapidly. The bum slumped down to the steps and the short man's right arm followed the lowering face, smashing into it with a swinging arc and the steady action of a trip hammer. The bum sprawled flat on the pavement and the man began kicking his head with the same rapid movement. Windows flung open in the tenement above and at the sound of the screams and shouts the short man walked very quickly away, disappearing into the dark, followed by the man with the cigarette. The bum held his head, staring at the small, dirty pool of blood on the steps. A large, gray-haired woman in the window directly above wrung her hands and shouted,

"They didn't need to do it — he wasn't hurting anything. Oh my God — don't you know? They did it because he was white!" A man behind her in the window said, "Oh for God's sake, come on." The window slammed shut, and the street again was quiet.

A young father, born into this world by parents who came from the narrow and settled streets of San Juan, explained the neighborhood violence.

"You even get used to it, man. It don't get to you unless it's someone right in the family who's the one that gets hurt. There isn't as much gang fighting now as there used to be but it still goes on, and so does the regular killing, besides the gang stuff. People think all that stuff was over in the twenties with machine guns shooting out of cars and all that, but it's still really here — it's just got more under cover. You can still get a guy killed anytime. You hire a kid who's high and you promise him a fix. For a fix, he'll do anything. Then if you want to make sure nobody knows about it afterward you give him an overdose and that does it. They call it suicide."

A mother who lives in the neighborhood agreed, and added, "Yes, there are times when you see a car pull up, and they push out a girl all beat up and her clothes torn. After a while you get used to seeing it — violence. The thing you learn, the first thing you learn is, 'I didn't see anything.' No matter where you were or what happened, you didn't see anything."

Sometimes the people who live in it call East Harlem "The Jungle," and that is its law — you didn't see anything. When you really don't see it, you hear about it later. There is always a story of violence past or the threat of violence to come. Some people make a living from it, and some make a living from its by-product — fear. For several years in the forties the neighborhood was plagued by the Batman. The Batman appeared on roofs of tenements, stretching his great black arms, extending his terrible claws, and then running off to another roof or down a fire escape — some people swore he flew away. He robbed apartments, and the times that brave souls gave him chase he stopped and stretched out his wing-like arms, and few men were ready to follow. Parents told children that the Batman would come off the roofs and carry them away if they were bad. Once the police saw the Batman and finally caught him — not a bat at all but a man with a large imagination and a large black cloak and two small garden rakes with clawlike prongs. Every American neighborhood has its imaginary witches, its Batman summoned by mothers to discipline the kids — but in Harlem the Batman is real. He really appears, and adults do not chase him.

Nor do adults chase the kids of the teen-age gangs. The gangs in many ways are born of the neighborhood fear, and they compound it, leaving their own particular scars, inside and out. Alicia, the thirteen-year-old daughter of Providencia, came once, confused, to ask a friend's advice about a girl who was living in terror of a gang. The girl, Alicia's friend in school, had been going out with a boy from a gang. One night she went out with a boy from up the street who was not in the gang. The old boy friend's gang came and got her and took her to the East River and picked her up and said they were going to throw her in. She screamed and cried and they put her down, but told her that if she wasn't careful they would get her again and really throw her in the river.

"She is sick all the time now," Alicia said. "She's scared they'll throw her in the river, and she gets all out of breath sometimes, like she's having a heart attack or something."

The grownups understand that these kids are different from other kids. A man stood across the street from the silver-and-black-painted storefront that marks the home of The Conservatives Club, watching the boys go in for pool, and said, as if in admission and discovery, "You know, we call them kids, just because they happen to be a certain age — fourteen, or fifteen, or sixteen — but they're not kids. They've seen too much."

This was the essence of the difficult decision the gang made to give up fighting and become Conservatives — they had seen too much. Many of them were members of an old and greatly feared gang called The Enchanters. In the fall of 1956 the simple fact was that all the old leaders were either dead, in jail, in Riverside narcotics hospital, or had moved away. A few of the oldest veterans who were left (ages seventeen and eighteen) found themselves leaders by virtue of survival. Their first concern was continued survival, for the gang was greatly weakened and rival gangs of the neighborhood were still strong. An eighteen-year-old boy named Monk Wescott and several other weary veterans decided that the best thing to do was give up fighting and go social. But the problem then was how to do it.

Monk and several other veterans went to Ramón Diaz, the man who came in his early twenties, about eight years ago, to the mainland on a Bahai pilgrimage to Chicago, stopped off in New York on the way, and still hasn't left. Ramón is a man on the block who always has answers, and the boys went to him in hopes of finding one for their dilemma. Ramón has since been called a social worker but that is misleading. Social workers go to school to get a degree in the mysteries of dealing with people; Ramón was born with that degree. He has worked on and off around the neighborhood as a helper in a law office, a furniture store, and a campaign for the state assembly, and he soon became a familiar figure — not so much for whatever work it was he happened to be doing but rather for the fact that he "knew everyone." Wherever he happens to be, Ramón is The Insider. He moves through the neighborhood always in a hurry but always at ease, and his high-cheeked, light tan face — usually topped with a natty cap that he is quick to tip to the ladies — breaks quite readily into a broad, white smile.

When the guys from The Enchanters asked Ramón to help them figure out how to go social, Ramón took it with a grain of salt. He had been around. "I told them go way — you guys don't mean it." But they kept on pestering Ramón and pleading with him. He asked them why they wanted to change, and one of them explained, "We are in so many troubles." Finally Ramón went to Norman Eddy and asked if the gang could use the 100th Street church of the East Harlem Protestant Parish for some meetings to discuss going social. The request was granted, though against the wishes of some of the members of the church, who knew the gang's history and had little faith in its future intentions.

The Enchanters began in the postwar era of growing teen-age gang activity throughout New York. In the early fifties they had a total of seven "divisions" in the neighborhood, grouped according to age — beginning from nine and going to twenty, with classifications such as Tiny Tots, Mighty Mites, Juniors, and Seniors. Their legend and influence spread not only through the ages of the neighborhood kids but also outward through the other parts of New York and across the river into Jersey. Branches of The Enchanters were found in the Bronx, in Brooklyn, in Hoboken; their lower Manhattan arm still exists as one of the most active fighting gangs in the city. As one grown veteran explained the days of power, "Man, The Enchanters weren't a gang — they were an organization." A member could pass in acceptance to many far worlds in that era of empire. The eighteen-year-old leader, Count Benny, on 103rd Street was Caesar in a slum-scarred Rome.

The empire's boundaries reached to new territory, not only geographically but socially. The Enchanters were the first of the gangs in the area to extend their membership past the limits of a single racial or national group. Though composed mainly of Puerto Ricans, The Enchanters had Negroes and several Italians in their organization. A former Enchanter, now the head of a family, recalled that this was a radical departure: "The gangs used to be strictly according to whether you were a Puerto Rican or an Italian or something like that. Now, you hear all this talk about Italian gangs and Puerto Rican gangs, but it's not all one way or the other. The Italian gang that's left up north has maybe twenty guys who are Puerto Ricans. It's not so much that stuff now as it is cliques — which clique is strongest. That's different than it was. Ten years ago I couldn't walk down 105th Street or I'd get it because I was a Spic."

When the Puerto Rican colony formed in East Harlem, and as it began to grow, the fear among the old Italian, Jewish, and Irish inhabitants became articulated into the message that "the Puerto Ricans are taking over — they are running us out." The parents said it and the kids absorbed it. Boundaries then were strictly defined, with certain blocks "belonging" to Italians, some to Negroes, and some to Puerto Ricans. For years, no Puerto Ricans went to the only public swimming pool in the area because it "belonged" to the Italians. The new boys were enemies, threatening tenement house and hearth. Gangs "defended" their neighborhood against the encroachers by beating them up. And, in protection, the newcomers organized to fight the tormenters.

The pattern is nothing new to Manhattan. The only things that change are the neighborhoods and the old nationalities. The first recorded gang in New York City was formed in a grocery store on Center Street in 1825, and since that time there have always been gangs. The first gangs were Irish, exclusive not only in national but sometimes city and county origins. One was made up of members who all came from County Kerry, and called themselves, on the new strange streets of New York, The Kerryonians.

But that is forgotten history now. Since the latest strangers to the city are from Puerto Rico, the belief is widely held that all contemporary civic evils, including gangs, come from Puerto Rico — perhaps packed into the flimsy suitcases carried off the planes from San Juan that land at Idlewild airport. But there still are no teen-age fighting gangs in Puerto Rico. No boy ever came to New York from the island wearing the silken jacket of a gang — he finds it here, and buys it by necessity. The Enchanters' social ancestors were not from San Juan but from County Kerry.

A reporter named Herbert Asbury wrote that:

the gangster whose reign ended with the murder of Kid Dropper was primarily a product of his environment; poverty and disorganization of home and community brought him into being, and political corruption and all its attendant evils fostered his growth. He generally began as a member of a juvenile gang, and lack of proper direction and supervision naturally graduated him into the ranks of older gangsters. Thus he grew to manhood without the slightest conception of right and wrong, with an aversion to honest labor that amounted to actual loathing and with a keen admiration for the man who was able to get much for nothing. Moreover, his only escape from the misery of his surroundings lay in excitement, and he could imagine no outlet for his turbulent spirit save sex and fighting. And many a boy became a gangster solely because of an overwhelming desire to emulate the exploits of some spectacular figure of the underworld, or because of a yearning for fame and glory which he was unable to satisfy except by acquiring a reputation as a tough guy and hard mug.

The gangsters referred to are those who reached their flower in the latter part of the nineteenth century in New York City, and whose gangs lived on until the late 1920's. The description is from Asbury's book, *The Gangs of New York*, published in 1928. The names are different but the phrases still fit: "Poverty and disorganization of home and community brought him into being, and political corruption and all its attendant evils fostered his growth . . . his only escape from the misery of his surroundings lay in excitement, and he could imagine no outlet for his turbulent spirit save sex and fighting . . . " The only difference is that the old system of teen-age gangs graduated its members into adult extensions, for when the grown-up gangs were low on members because of death, jail, or defection, they called up recruits from the juvenile gangs.

One of the few distinctions so far between the Puerto Ricans and the early immigrant groups to New York is that the Puerto Ricans have developed no criminal gangs of adults as the Irish, Jews, and Italians did. This is perhaps a happy fact for the social workers, but may in the long run be a sad one for the progress of the Puerto Ricans. Many old-time observers in the city believe that this lack of an adult underworld is one of the reasons why the Puerto Ricans have not yet achieved any power in politics. Whatever the merits of the case may be, the Puerto Rican kid who grows out of a teen-age gang cannot go on to membership in a Puerto Rican criminal gang of adults because there are none. He more likely goes on into the adult social club that often develops from his gang after the members are married and settled.

This was what happened with María Flores and many of her friends from 110th Street, whose neighborhood teen-age gang called The Senecas became The Manhattan Seneca Social Club, Inc. The Senecas rent a small, narrow basement room on 110th Street, which the members have furnished with a juke box, a bar at the back where drinks can be purchased for 35¢, formal pictures of the group, and a framed certificate of incorporation. On Friday and Saturday nights a member and the friends he brings may stop in for dancing, drinks, and talk. One of the members is posted at the door to see that only those people known and in good standing may enter.

"We just allow the ones who are doing all right," María said. "Nobody in narcotics or rackets can belong. Mostly it's the old bunch that started the gang when we were ten years old. You know, you have to form a gang like that to protect yourself when you go on other blocks. Now we take in younger people too, but mostly it's the same ones who used to live around 110th when I was growing up. We have parties and all that, and when one of us is in any trouble we try to help him out, take up collections if anyone needs a loan bad, or something like that."

Gathered together as children to defend themselves, the grown-up Senecas still look out for one another. That motive for the birth of a gang is nothing new — as indeed, few things are new about the gangs of New York today. When Asbury talks of the gangs of a century before — their need for escape from the misery of surroundings and their yearning for fame and glory — he talks about The Enchanters. The name of the gang expresses its hope and highest promise.

Names are of great importance, and the name of The Enchanters was one of the biggest issues in the gang's debate about going social. When a kid becomes a member of a fighting or "bopping" gang, or when his gang decides to start fighting, the member changes the way he walks. A gang member can watch a guy walk down the street and tell you whether he is bopping or not. A bopping gang that was going social obviously needed a different name to signify the change. The majority decided on "Conservatives" but there was stiff opposition.

The meetings to discuss the change were attended by the boys and girls who belonged to The Enchanters, several guys from the rival Dragons and Comanches gangs who were interested in going social, and Ramón Diaz, acting as an informal adviser. The sessions were stormy, with some of the old Enchanters walking out, and others arguing that changing the name would mean a betrayal of the gang's great history.

The girls were among the strongest opponents of changing the name. Many of them used to date Enchanters who were now in jail or in the hospital and they felt that in respect to those boys and the gang's tradition the name should stay the same. When sentiment began to grow for the "Conservatives," the girls proposed a compromise name: "The Conservative E's."

But retaining some letter of the past meant more than just respect for the old boy friends and heroes. It meant retaining some spirit of the past. And many of the girls were anxious to do that. Disputes over girls are often the excuse for starting a gang war, and girls are not always displeased by this. The girl whose honor or love is in question rarely runs any risk of physical injury herself, and the glamour of being fought over by whole gangs of boys has a powerful attraction. If the new Conservatives gave up fighting altogether the girls would not be as important as they were in the days when their glances could start a war. It was over the opposition of most of the girls that the boys who favored going social were eventually able to eliminate the "E" and name the new club — simply and profoundly — The Conservatives.

During the great debate about the name and purpose of the club a dozen or so of the old Enchanters left in disgust and disillusionment about the new peaceful plans. Some joined gangs in the area that were still bopping, and some just stayed on their own. At the same time, Ramón Diaz was influencing the group to bring in new, younger members who were not a part of the old tradition. This was a great help in shaping the club's new course to conservatism. But the course was not yet certain.

The biggest and most precarious step was taken when the guys agreed to give up all their old "pieces" — their guns. This unilateral disarmament meant that if other gangs didn't respect the change, the Conservatives would be without an arsenal to defend themselves.

The gang had no sooner emptied its arsenal when a challenge came from the rival Dragons. Some of the old Enchanters bitterly regretted having given up their arms. Monk Wescott, one of the veterans who had first asked Ramón Diaz for help in going social, was torn between the challenge of the peace and the challenge of the Dragons.

When the time had come to give up the pieces, some guys sold them (many gangs keep a special treasury for purchase of arms) and some took the safer course of throwing them into the river. Monk and several of the others had buried theirs in a basement.

In the last minutes of the Dragon challenge, when the Dragons were on their way to 100th Street, Monk and several others uncovered the buried pieces, went to the roof of a housing project, and fired down at the enemy. The police had been notified and quickly spotted the boys and arrested them. Monk and one other boy were charged with attempted assault and sentenced to what is known in the neighborhood as a "zip five" — a maximum five years at the state correctional institution at Comstock, New York, with the final determination of dismissal to be made by the authorities of the institution on the basis of behavior there.

With another of the few remaining veterans gone, the gang would be even weaker in any future fighting. Monk's departure made going social seem even more vital and yet at the same time it proved again the difficulties of a gang on the streets of the neighborhood in staying out of trouble. The members understood that they needed more than a new name to insure a permanent peace.

Many of them felt that if they only had a place to go — a place of their own where they could enter and shut out the world of adults and enemies and strangers — they would have a better chance of holding to the nonfighting way of life. Their meeting place had always been a candy store, which is usually the closest thing to a home that a gang in East Harlem can expect.

But a candy store, like a community center, is ruined by the fact that it is open to the public. At best it's a place to hang around, and better than no place at all. When The Enchanters were not on the street they hung around in the candy store owned by a woman called La Vieja — the Old Lady. She got to know the guys and served them, as well as other people from the block, with candy, cigarettes, and sandwiches, whether or not they had the price at the time of purchase. A box was kept on the counter for contributions, and those who were broke merely took what they needed and then, when they got a job or money from the family, they paid what they figured they owed to the box. In this way La Vieja conducted her business and made her living through the most "unsocial" days of The Enchanters. Only once was money stolen from the box of contributions, and the thief was caught and soundly beaten by the rest of the gang.

As a candy store, La Vieja's was fine, but The Conservatives wanted something more. The idea of a clubhouse had been brought up before and now became a main topic of the meetings. Ramón Diaz was asked to find out if there was any possibility of getting one, and Ramón went again to Reverend Eddy. Norm was by this time impressed with the gang's determination to go social and was anxious to give it any impetus possible. He remembered discussing the problem with a woman from a midtown youth foundation who was interested in having her group, the Kips Bay Boys Club, give some support to youth work in East Harlem. Norm got in touch with her again, and sent Ramón Diaz with a delegation of Conservatives to talk with the ladies.

They worked out an arrangement for the Kips Bay foundation to contribute to the support of a clubhouse and the hiring of a full-time director for the Conservatives. Ramón Diaz was chosen as the salaried adult director, and the store on First Avenue was rented for a clubhouse. The boys were to help pay the rent, through dues and money-raising projects, and the sponsors would match any sum the boys were able to raise to help buy equipment and furnishings. Ramón and the officers were to meet once a month with the ladies to report on finances and activities of the club. The members fixed up the clubhouse and each Conservative dipped his hand in silver paint and pressed the print of his palm on the wall to signify commitment to the new way of life. It was a mass voluntary fingerprinting that hopefully meant the end of a need for required fingerprinting in the future. The clubhouse was further equipped with tables and chairs, a pool table, a radio, and the large silver sign that insured the privacy that had never been: "Members Only."

Membership now meant something different. Rules were adopted that required a member to be either in school or working, or to give the club a reason why he wasn't. Ramón began helping members get jobs, through local contacts and the U.S. Employment Service. The new rules also required that no member could be a member of another gang, nor be caught fighting or using drugs. New members would have to go through a four-week probationary period to see if they would abide by the rules of the club. Then their acceptance would have to be by unanimous vote.

Since the final change in the name and purpose of the club, in the spring of 1957, it has held to its course, lost a few members, and gained more new ones. Among the new ones are recruits from other gangs, including Georgie Baez, former "war lord" of the Dragons, and Tito Camacho, a former war lord of the Latin Gents. Except for one attack in the days of evolution, the other gangs have, for the most part, left the Conservatives alone. The first real period of trial — the long and always dangerous summer when streets are full and the gangs are restless — passed without a war. The Conservatives stayed around the clubhouse, clinging to the new way of life that often seemed supported by only a thread, a pool cue, and the memory of "so many troubles" in the past.

One night, which was every night, the guys were inside playing pool beneath the neon light and the blare of the radio that drowned the room in the rhythm of rock'n'roll. The sound poured out the open door and onto the street and the sidewalk, where a few guys paced back and forth in the complicated patterns of idleness, sat down on the folding chairs in front of the clubhouse, got up again, went inside, and drifted back out — only to return to the light. Bobby Montesi, the club's president, a short, lean boy who is seen in all seasons with a blue beret, stopped in the pattern of his tracks next to George, a ramrod-tall, thin Negro boy, who was also pacing the night. They had passed on their ways in and out of the clubhouse several times without any notice, but this time they stopped, as if their wandering routes had been planned to lead to this particular point all evening. They leaned close together and Bobby struck a note that harmonized with the rock'n'roll song inside. His face lifted and stretched in concentration toward the note. George's head bent down on his sweatshirt, reaching for a deeper note that underlined the one that Bobby still held. They struck a harmony the radio had already left behind, and they heard the blare no longer, now absorbed in their own music. Kenny, who was balanced against the front of the club on a tilted chair, got up, letting it click to the cement, and leaned into the harmony. Bobby drew the folded newspaper from under his arm and extended it still in front of him to serve as a baton. The chord was stretched, and then Bobby whipped the paper upward and the voices rose with it. The hum turned into a "doo-ah, doo-ah" that carried itself ahead, doubled back, and concluded, long and low. The folded paper baton that Bobby held now below his waist, as if pressing down the final chord that threatened to burst from its own power, suddenly lowered to Bobby's side and the three guys walked away again without a word, continuing their own special routes. George still whistled the memory of the tune they had made. The others were silent.

Five or six girls outside the clubhouse screeched in unison as two of the boys came down the block. The boys ignored them in a sure, studied manner, chewing harder on their gum and running their hands up their bright suspenders, and sauntered inside to the more serious business of the pool table. The girls, after scattering in laughter, gathered again on the stoop of the building beside the clubhouse, chattering, peeping inside, and staring down the street to see who might come next.

The short, gold-skinned girl called "Tiny" whose love had promoted several battles in the past and continual personal fights among rivals, leaned against a handsome, half-embarrassed boy, who in turn was leaning against a parked car, and bent down to kiss her as she raised her face in quick, teasing darts that were almost kisses and left too soon. The other girls didn't watch. On the stoop they talked of the imminent terror of school, starting the talk in English and often, when excited, switching to Spanish and ending in high, long laughter.

A girl in black toreador pants and an orange sweater slipped off the cement stoop and turned to ask the others, as if she had just remembered, "Hey, did you kids see that stage show at the Paramount? Fats Domino?"

The other girls shrieked their approval.

"Yeh," said one, "and that movie though — with that band playing that American dance music — you see the way they go?"

The girl stepped out on the sidewalk, held her arm up stiffly in fox-trot position, and moved slowly in a wandering box step with a sour expression on her face. The others laughed. "American" music, which is any besides the Spanish and Latin American dances and rock'n'roll, is painfully square and wholly lost between the extremes of the dance as practiced at the Friday night canteens attended by Conservatives at the Family Center of the Parish on 100th Street.

It is this event, supplemented occasionally by Saturday night dances sponsored by the Conservatives in the same place and with nearly the same faces, that alone serves to break the routine of pool, pacing, and rock'n'roll that sustains the club through its new, nonviolent life.

In the past the canteens were often a part of the violence. Being the only teen-age social occasions in the neighborhood, they grew with boys and girls and gangs from all around, hundreds of kids pressing into the dusty hall of the Family Center on 100th Street and the basement of the Parish church on 106th Street, where a record dance canteen was also held. A member of the church staff and a member of the police force were always present, but in the swelling evenings, with rival gang members facing off in challenges through the patterns of the crowds, there was no way to keep control. Sometimes guns were smuggled in, at first for show and then for action. A boy was shot and killed in the canteen on 106th Street and that was the last canteen for the street.

On 100th Street, however, new measures were taken to keep down the crowds, parents were brought in as well as police, and the Parish, fearing the worse kinds of trouble that could easily develop without any canteen at all, kept it going and kept it orderly. There have also been shootings at the 100th Street canteen in the past, but in the last year all has been relatively quiet. A great new factor for peace has been The Conservatives.

They come now, boys and girls in separate, clustering groups with occasionally a couple, dancing, clapping and singing beneath the glow of fluorescent lights made colorful and dim by crepe-paper wrappings. Sometimes a boy will be dressed in a new Ivy League style suit, shoes shined to a brilliant gloss, perhaps even wearing what constitutes the final touch of full dress — dark glasses. More often they are dressed in bright-striped sport shirts and khaki or denim pants, with, from time to time, the particular fad of the moment, which was for a while the bright strips of cloth wrapped turban fashion around the boys' heads and set with a flashy piece of jewelry rummaged from home.

The music blares loud and fast, in rock'n'roll or Latin rhythm, and always the time comes when one of the girls waves a hand and four or five other girls follow in a line behind her, keeping the complicated steps she leads with, as the rest of the crowd backs off to watch. The "meringue" is a favorite; but fast music finally stops, and one of the slow rock'n'roll tunes that drags in thick, halting harmony fills the room, and the boys are standing by girls. Couples embrace, and it is then the duty of the attendant minister to see that the practiced technique of this dance is "fish" and not "grind." If the feet are moving, it is fish and legal; if the only movement is in the bodies that are, in either case, pressed together, it is grind and the offenders will be tapped on the shoulder and asked to start fishing again.

So goes the evening, from fast, blaring rhythm to slow, blaring fish, and occasional communal singing with the record. At eleven o'clock it is over, and the kids return to the street. Boys without girls may go to a candy store and gather at the juke box for still more music; some seek the shelter of hallways to work out their own singing arrangements. The Conservatives have their own official singing group, called The Persuaders, and there are many others throughout the neighborhood. The rock'n'roll singing group is the only quick and legal outlet that kids in East Harlem hold as a vision of escape to overnight fame and riches. The many teen-age groups that have suddenly made the list of national record and stage stars — many of them out of Harlem — provide a fabulous goal for the kids. Much as the boys in the slums of Spain and Mexico gather in dusty lots to practice the art of the matador with homemade capes and sticks for swords in the hope of a sudden path to wealth and success, the kids of East Harlem gather in tenement hallways to practice their harmony.

The kids who leave the canteen dances with dates may go to the hallways too — but not to sing. There is of course no such thing as "getting the family car" for "a drive in the country." Necking has to be done in the hallways. For more serious

sexual adventures, the refuge is the roof. This can be dangerous, for there are often older adventurers strolling the rooftops — but the kids rarely find another place to be alone.

Whatever the after-the-dance adventure, there is always, at
last, the return to the street; the last place to linger before going back to an overcrowded tenement room. Tomorrow there
will be the clubhouse again, and next week, again, the dance.

The question among the oldtimers on the block was whether
this schedule, when the new routine got old, would be enough
to keep The Conservatives conservative. Louie, a small, finely
featured boy from the block, who left it for the army, already
a veteran of the wars of The Enchanters, returned on leave
and criticized the old gang — not for turning conservative but
rather for not doing it with more imagination.

"This," he judged, "is not enough." As a former Enchanter
he was interested in what had come to pass and anxious that it
not pass back to what had been. He had almost been ruined
in its violence, and left the block to enlist after coming close
to prison for his part in a gang-war shooting — a fact quite
difficult to match with the face of the boy, which was only
saved by the faint dark trace of a mustache from being the
face of a child.

"What you guys need," he told one of the new Conservatives, "is a guy with ideas — a guy to say, 'Listen, let's get up
an outing' or 'Let's go up to a dance in the Bronx,' and then
have a few guys around who right quick say, 'Yeh, man, that's
a good idea.' You have the right guys to say it's a good idea,
and then everybody goes along, you know? The trouble with
you guys is you're just sitting around. You need to get out,
meet other people, see what it's like away from this neighborhood. It's hangin' around that gets you into trouble."

Victor, the young Conservative, pointed out weakly that they did have regular meetings.

"Meetings," said Louie. "Yeh, I went to that meeting. What kind of meeting was that? You just sat around and talked about dues."

Louie reached out his cupped hand, as if attempting to grab some tangible formula, and leaned across the table.

"What you have to do," he said, "is not to talk about who's paying dues, but what you're going to do with the dues money after you get it. That's the thing to talk about."

Victor stared at the table, considering, and looked up to say, "I tell you, Louie, I wish you were back on the block now."

Louie shrugged, sat back, and smiled.

"Now," he said. "Yeh, but it's a good thing I left when I did."

He was quiet for a moment, and then he said, "You know, they say the army makes a man of you. All the stuff you see and have to take. But those guys there, they haven't seen anything. I say 100th Street makes a man of you. The things I saw, I've got to thinking about, and I tell you, the guys at the base, they wouldn't believe it if I told 'em. I thought about writing a book, you know — but nobody'd read it."

He leaned back and laughed. "People see these movies and books about gangs and get to thinking that's the way it is. And most of it's phony. Just like this TV play we saw at the base, about a gang, it could never have happened. The way it was, they had some gang that wanted to take care of a kid, and so they dressed him up in their gang jacket and sent him into the territory of an enemy gang and the enemy gang saw the kid and beat him up. Well, you know, there's no gang that'd make a guy dress in their jacket when he wasn't a member —

it'd ruin the honor of the gang. They'd just take care of the kid themselves, that's all.

"And lots of these stories in magazines and books, they usually have some racketeer who comes along and sells them guns to make a big profit for himself and they start using guns then — like it's that one guy who turned 'em bad. Hell. It's never like that. If a gang wants pieces, it gets pieces — it gets 'em all kind of ways from all kind of places. It's not just one guy coming along and selling them the idea himself.

"The real things, the things that really happen, people would never believe. Just like the time, I'll never forget it — you weren't around here yet — we were up on a roof on 103rd Street shooting down at the Dragons. We came down off the roof and chased 'em down 104th Street, past the Precinct station — none of the cops even came out after us — ran down the next block and were shooting from doorsteps. One guy from the Dragons sneaked up on one of our guys and pointed a rifle straight at his head, and everything stopped, and the guy from the Dragons pulled the trigger and nothing happened. Our guy kept on pulling the trigger. I don't know why it didn't go off — it had been going off all right before. The guy finally figured it wasn't going off, and he walked away, and that was the end of it. Everyone just went home.

"That kind of thing would never have happened a few years before that though. I mean with the gun. Right after the war I remember I was just a little kid and guns first started showing up a lot, in the open. At first it was a real big deal. A guy would pull a gun in the street and everyone out on the block would scatter. Maybe it wasn't even loaded, maybe you couldn't hit a thing with it; all you had to do was pull a gun. Then, people got used to 'em, and after a while it got so a guy pulled a gun and another guy would just stand there and ask him, 'Well, you going to use that or not? You better use it or put it away.' That's the way it got to be. That's why now there's none of this waving a gun around and watching people run. You got to use it or put it away."

The wars of the street are not a game for boys, and the wars are not yet over. The transformation of Enchanters to Conservatives is not a large-scale revolution; it is rather the exception to the rule. The fighting gangs are still all around, and their action is an everyday concern.

It was, on a Sunday in hot July, the concern of the sermon at the 100th Street church of the East Harlem Protestant Parish, where the Reverend Norman Eddy preached on "Jesus and His Gang." That Friday night Norm had been more concerned with two gangs who had come to 100th Street to clash and were persuaded to meet to talk peace in the church with Norm as the mediator. He had left the canteen Friday night, his face set tense, and returned again an hour later, still walking fast, but smiling. One of the guys at the door of the canteen — a graduated veteran of gangs — had asked, "Hey Norm, is it over now?"

Norm started to nod and then he stopped, shrugged his shoulders, and said, "Is it ever really over?"

He prepared his sermon for Sunday on the "gang" of Jesus and the gangs of the neighborhood. Many of the new Conservatives attend the 100th Street church of the Parish, and they were in the uneasy trial of their first summer as a "social" instead of a "bopping" gang. But Norm was talking not only to them when he talked about the gangs. He was talking to everyone who lived in the neighborhood.

He said the teen-agers had it especially hard because they

had to decide on whether to get involved with the fighting.

"You have to make your decision," he said. "Most men and boys are afraid to be afraid. Not one of you here is outside of the problem. If you're a teen-ager and you're not in a club, you're still affected by it because you know when you walk to the subway whether another club is on the street, or in the candy store, and you know what is going on with them. When one of your friends is hurt, you want to defend him, and you get all mad inside, and yet something tells you it's wrong — but you're afraid to be afraid. You're afraid of being called a punk.

"But there is a special kind of courage — a real courage — that goes beyond that. It is the courage to stand up for God, and if you do that, maybe people will call you a punk for six months, but then finally they'll turn to you and look up to you. I know it's hard. When a club comes into the neighborhood with their pieces, it's hard.

"You girls, you're not outside of this either. In fact, it's often you that's in the middle. You're why the gang from farther uptown comes into the neighborhood — because you go with one of the guys. You have the chance to work between the gangs, for God."

Norm asked that the parents have understanding for their teen-age children and sympathy with what they must pass through to grow up within this neighborhood. Norm Eddy prayed for God to give them strength, and the congregation bowed in the prayer. From behind them came the noise of the street, always present, a constant chorus, to which they would rise up and go once more.

The street would be the same. The Conservatives have gone social and thereby changed their relation to society, but society is still as it was before. The pusher is still in the doorway and the bopping gang is still in the neighborhood. The same temptations are met every day, and the million factors that made the members of the club once fight continue to be a part of their life in the city's worst slum. Norm Eddy understood, as Louie did, that in the long run the kids must find something more than a new routine and a place to meet to keep them out of the troubles of the past. The Conservatives have wrung from society a clubhouse; but not a cause.

"We came from the island when I was a little girl, and I was in school. It was mostly Negroes and white children then and I wasn't either one. It was cold — oh Lord, it was cold in the winter — and I just had those short silk dresses we wore in Puerto Rico. I nearly froze, and I must have looked like a little refugee. I begged my grandmother to get me some leggings, and she said in Puerto Rico it wasn't right for girls to wear pants. I said but this isn't Puerto Rico, and she said that doesn't matter."

Opportunity

Surely Shakespeare is wicked, the map a bad example
With ships and sun and love tempting them to steal —
For lives that slyly turned in their cramped holes
From fog to endless night? On their slag heap, these children
Wear skins peeped through by bones and spectacles of steel
With mended glass, like bottle bits on stones.
All of their time and space and foggy slum
So blot their maps with slums as big as doom . . .

— "An Elementary School Classroom
in a Slum," STEPHEN SPENDER

P.S. 168, MANHATTAN, is a mammoth gray building whose grim exterior brings to mind neither the nostalgic image of the red brick, belfried schoolhouse of old, nor the plate-glass, single-story school of the new suburban America. Its appearance suggests some junior Bastille, and its reputation has earned it, along with the neighboring schools in East Harlem, the name of "Siberia" among the teachers who conduct its classes. Through its heavy portals pass the children of the slums. Once they were mostly Italians, Negroes, Jews, and Irish; now they are mostly Puerto Ricans.

The Reverend George Todd, a crew-cut young man with a stiff white collar, stood outside on the pavement opposite P.S. 168 one hot June day near the end of the term, and surveyed the blank, dirty face of the school. As minister of the 106th Street church of the East Harlem Protestant Parish he had listened long hours to complaints by parents who felt that their children were being cheated of a proper education; had listened, answerless, to questions of what could be done, and wondered what to believe of what he heard about the elementary school of the neighborhood. He had finally decided to see for himself. He made an appointment for a tour of the building, and arrived on the glaring June day with the sweat seeping through his gray shirt and forming above the firm rim of his collar. He studied briefly the image of the building's exterior and then walked briskly inside.

One of the school's two assistant principals welcomed the Reverend Todd to a seat by his desk in a spacious room whose plain school furniture failed to change the impression of vacancy. The room had a sense of transience about it, as if it were the office of a phantom corporation that might, overnight, move on and leave the building barren.

The assistant principal seemed more reassuring and solid than his immediate surroundings. He was a tall, wiry man with gray hair and glasses on a long, thin face that was lined and alert. His blue single-breasted business suit hung loosely on his slightly stooping frame, and his face, not his actions, suggested the weariness of school's last days on East 104th Street.

Only several years before, he had come to P.S. 168 from the staff of an elementary school in a well-to-do section of Queens. He told the Reverend Todd that he found fewer problems of discipline in the Harlem school than he had in his former post.

"There is all this talk about the Blackboard Jungle," he said, "but we don't get it here in the elementary grades. There is difficulty with gangs when they get older, but here the kids respect authority. The principal, the teachers, they're important people. In Queens, in a neighborhood like the one I was in, the kids are taught by the parents that the school is there to 'serve them'; the principal and teachers are 'public servants.' Well, you don't respect a servant. Here if a kid stays out of school a truant officer goes after him. In Queens if a kid stays out of school his parents get the family doctor to write a note that says he was sick, whether he was or not.

"The parents." The assistant principal smiled. "Out there, it was the parents that gave us so much trouble. Here, of course, we seldom hear from the parents."

But all this was not to say that P.S. 168 was without its particular problems.

"The most trouble in discipline seems to be among the kids themselves, mainly between the Puerto Ricans and the Negroes. You might expect it would be between the whites and the Puerto Ricans, or whites and Negroes, but that doesn't seem to be the main problem in our school. The principal found that it was better to have separation in classes — Puerto Ricans in one section, the rest in another — for these social as well as educational reasons. A fight between a Puerto Rican and another boy was liable to carry on from the playground to the classroom. But if the Puerto Ricans are kept in separate classes, they come into class and the fight's all over.

"Also, our principal found it was better from the standpoint of learning to read and write that the kids be separated. If the children don't know English, you teach them reading and writing English in a different way than you would teach children who speak English already."

The assistant principal drew a battered pack of cigarettes from the pocket of his shirt, lit one, and blew a long, relieving stream of smoke toward the window.

"That's the way it was worked out here, according to experience," he said. "But it's not being done like that right now. You see, there was a policy recently instituted of extra state appropriations for schools with classes having fifty per cent or more Spanish-speaking enrollment. Actually it was for classes with fifty per cent or more 'foreign language' enrollment, but Spanish is of course what they mean. Now, the more classes you have with fifty per cent or more Puerto Ricans, the more appropriation money you get, so we've had to switch our classes all around and make a lot of changes to work it out to the best advantage. We now have close to sixty per cent Puerto Rican students out of our whole enrollment of about fifteen hundred students — five years ago we only had twenty per cent Puerto Ricans — and we have twenty-six out of sixty-one classes with fifty per cent or more Spanish-speaking children. In these classes, the children have to be taught all together, and we don't think that's the best system, but we feel the best thing is to get more money to be able to do more things for the schools, and that's the best way to help the children. Maybe later on they'll change this about the appropriations.

"Right now we have one teacher who can speak Spanish — she's a Negro herself and she likes the Puerto Rican kids, so of course we give them to her in classes — but the principal doesn't want her speaking Spanish to them in class. None of our teachers speak Spanish in class. Our principal thinks the best way is to have nothing but English spoken and read in the school — after all, they come to school to learn English. We have two other Spanish-speaking teachers who are substitutes, but they don't usually work with the classes. Their main job is to work with the parents when the parents can't speak English and the children are in some sort of difficulty or there are things wrong at home."

The Reverend Todd wondered what the teachers did at first with children who couldn't speak English and couldn't understand what was happening in class.

"In that case, they just have to wait till they pick it up — and in the meantime, if there is something urgent to tell the child, the teacher gets one of the other children to translate. There are always children in the class who can speak both Spanish and English."

The assistant principal stopped speaking and glanced at his watch. He said it was almost time for an auditorium program in celebration of Flag Day. He thought Reverend Todd would be interested in watching the children perform, and suggested that they sit in for the entertainment before making a tour of the classrooms.

Inside the huge auditorium the students of Class 6-2 (a designation that, in the complex terminology of P.S. 168, signifies the brightest class of the sixth grade) stood in the rows of folding chairs at the front, watching the swinging hand of a woman in a bright green dress who was tracing invisible patterns in the air as the children sang in high, cracking tone to "Largo," "Tru-ust i-in Goddddd . . ."

A small, dark-faced boy in a fresh white shirt darted quickly back to the assistant principal and handed him a crayon-colored program: "We Love the Flag: Class 6-2."

A kind of Greek chorus identified as "storytellers" assembled on the platform to chant the question that the program would try to answer: "What can there be in this flag that stirs men's hearts?"

Eleanor Espinola, a chubby little girl with straight black hair walked quickly, determinedly, to the center of the small stage, faced the auditorium squarely, and said in a high tone of near desperation, "I am Betsy Ross . . ."

And she proceeded to recount her (Miss Ross's) adventures with the Flag. Louis Medina, a tiny, curly-haired boy, announced himself as Thomas Jefferson and reported, without the slightest trace of nostalgia, that "I remember a sunny afternoon in 1776 . . ." and concluded by reading from his doctrine that "all men are created equal."

Eddie Vázquez, a serious bronze-faced boy dressed in khaki, told the audience that he was a U.S. Marine, that he died in Korea, and that the flag meant for him "the dignity of man."

The assistant principal, smiling, led the visiting minister out through the back of the hall while the chorus chanted its concluding affirmation of the dignity of man. The assistant principal explained, as he led Reverend Todd down the long, empty corridor, that the class they were about to visit was an "opportunity" class, consisting of "holdovers," children with emotional problems and Puerto Ricans. The holdovers, he continued, were children who had trouble with reading tests or I.Q. tests or both; the Puerto Ricans, unless they knew English well before coming to school, of course had trouble with reading.

Reverend Todd wondered if I.Q. tests were given to Puerto Rican children, and if so, how their language problem was taken into account in scoring their intelligence.

"For a while," the assistant principal explained, "they tried giving I.Q. tests in Spanish to the Puerto Rican kids, but that wasn't fair either, because most of them knew a little English and it was all mixed up in their mind. They were actually illiterate in two languages. Now, we just let the individual teachers judge the I.Q. of these children until they're far enough along to take the tests in English. You can usually judge. You can't get it right on the nose, of course, but you can pretty well judge what group they ought to be with."

In addition to the "opportunity" classes, the assistant principal explained that the school has another special category called "health" classes. The system of designation is, if nothing else, consistent. Opportunity classes are for those who have no opportunity; health classes are for those who are not in good health.

"The health classes have children of three main groups," the assistant principal said. "Orthopedics, cardiacs, and children of low vitality. Those with low vitality are suffering from malnutrition to a point damaging their capabilities of school performance. These we try to build up, talk to the parents about diet, and hopefully, eventually, move them out of the class. The orthopedics include cerebral palsy, post-polio, and various injury cases."

Reverend Todd and the assistant principal entered one of the "health" classes and were greeted by a bulky lady, who clasped her hands together and wrinkled her face at the pleasure of introduction. She beamed across her crippled classroom and called forth from the back a girl named Lola. Lola hobbled forward with one good leg and the other in a cast. One arm was bent, and shorter than the other. She stopped in front of the teacher, and the teacher reached down to part the little girl's hair and display an area of baldness to the visitors.

"Little Lola has just had an operation for a brain tumor," the teacher brightly explained, pointing to the bald spot on the child's head. "They had to take some skin away that shortened her little arm."

Gently, beaming, the teacher held up the shortened stub of the girl's left arm. She eased it back into place and then bent down to the child's leg, pointing, to say, "And even from her little leg."

She patted Lola on the head again, smoothing the hair across the bald spot, and Lola hobbled back to her seat.

The Reverend Todd thought he had perhaps taken enough of the assistant principal's time, and they returned to the silent office. The assistant principal, in the heat of the oncoming noon, removed his coat and took out another cigarette.

"You can see," he said, "there are many problems. And many aren't obvious, either. One of the biggest is turnover. Many of the parents are constantly moving. If they move four blocks away they are likely to be in another school district — the neighborhood is that heavily populated. Also there are the housing projects, and when the old houses are torn down it means a whole movement of hundreds of families. Some move out of the neighborhood altogether, and then when the new projects go up there's a whole set of new students moving in. And in September there's always a big influx from Puerto Rico. The sugar cane season is over and a lot of them have the money to come and be here when school opens in the fall. There's always a lot who are only here for a little while and go back to Puerto Rico again. And of course, those who come up from Puerto Rico and are already in school have done different work in their school down there."

The assistant principal paused, and the Reverend Todd got

up, thanking him for all his trouble and the information. He agreed that indeed there were complicated problems.

Down the stairs and through the long corridors the Reverend Todd walked slowly, looking at the posters and signs that were made by the children and put on display — brightly colored slogans that cheerfully, boldly, defied the facts of the world, the neighborhood, that waited outside:

> "Nature is all around us."
> "The Milkman brings us milk."
> "The Policeman is our friend."
> "Spring is here."

The school bears little relationship to the streets around it, where the policeman is the killer of Georgie Martínez, the milkman a legend of an older era of brownstone fronts and horse-drawn carts whose product is now too expensive for many of the families who live here largely on water and rice and beans. The children fed with those staples may qualify for the "health" class, where they take home lists of diets that are often impossible to fulfill. Alicia Robles and two of her brothers, all "health" class students, could describe the truth of their own lives better with a poster proclaiming: "We can't stand to eat from the jars of fat that the people at the hospital gave us to help our malnutrition." The truth is not fit for children's posters — only for children's lives.

The schools have been of little help to the children of Spanish Harlem in escaping the realities of its streets, or of changing those realities to something like the promise of the posters that smile from the classrooms. The schools, in fact, have blocked out the possibilities of the world beyond even more profoundly than the tenement buildings around them. The case of "Manny," the father who wants to go to school and study agriculture — but first has to learn to read and write in the evenings after his laboring job because he was pushed through and out of the neighborhood schools without those basic skills — is not an unusual or isolated case. The kids of average intelligence or above average intelligence who can barely cope with the basic uses of the English language when they get out of school are not the exceptions but the rule in this community. The roots of the tragedy reach back hundreds of years.

Education for the people of the Spanish-speaking island of Puerto Rico, taken over by an English-language country, has an old and painful history. It goes far beyond and dates much before the dilemmas of the schools in New York City. P.S. 168 was built in 1898; the same year, American troops marched into San Juan to take Puerto Rico from Spain, and soon after the troops arrived American schoolteachers followed. They found that the government of Spain had not been overly concerned about the education of the people who lived on this far-out possession. Only one building on the entire island had been specifically constructed for use as a school. Only 8 per cent of the children of school age were enrolled in any school, and only 15 per cent of all Puerto Ricans over ten years of age could read and write.

The U.S. military governor set up a bureau of education and ruled that all children from six to eighteen years of age were to be entitled to free education. Teachers were brought in from the U.S. mainland — few of whom had any knowledge of the Spanish language.

Transformation did not come easily. It was only two years

later that the military governor wondered about the wisdom of a widespread educational effort. The governor, George W. Davis, after getting to know his way around the poverty-stricken island, is reported to have felt — in the best Kiplingesque tradition — that perhaps education would only make the people want things they couldn't have. Let the natives remain in peace and ignorance. "Mistah Kurtz" didn't die in the heart of darkness; he had never arrived.

But despite the colonial qualms of Governor Davis, education in Puerto Rico forged ahead. It was, of course, strictly "American." The first U.S. commissioner of education in Puerto Rico reported with pride that because of his efforts the average Puerto Rican school child knew more about Washington, Lincoln, and Betsy Ross than the average mainland school child did. Furthermore, since Puerto Rico was now a U.S. possession, the only "logical" thing to do was conduct all classes in the English language on this island that for four hundred years had spoken only Spanish. Children entering the first grade were as familiar with English as they were with Arabic, yet they were expected to learn reading, writing, arithmetic, history, and science from teachers speaking in English, many of whom were straight from the mainland and knew not a word of Spanish. The core of former Puerto Rican teachers were not allowed to go on teaching their classes in Spanish; they had to learn English and teach with it. This massive, self-styled Berlitz system resulted largely in chaos rather than education.

The system was maintained until 1930 when a Puerto Rican, Dr. José Padín, was appointed Commissioner of Education on the island. He reformed the whole educational process to a method whereby all subjects in elementary school were taught in Spanish, and English was taught as a required subject. This allowed the students to learn their lessons as well as learn English, and met with great approval and relief from the people of the island. It did not, of course, manage to transform Puerto Rico into an English-speaking or a bilingual island in a few years' time. But it had only a few years' time of trial.

In 1936 the small, terrorist, Nationalist party of Puerto Rico lashed out against American possession of the island by a series of assassinations and attacks, and Washington turned a new and troubled eye on its Caribbean outpost. Senator William H. King of Utah, head of the Senate Committee on Territories, was dispatched to Puerto Rico to investigate the situation. He quickly sensed that the anti-American violence must be due to the fact that the islanders spoke a foreign language. The story of King's investigative visit has been well told by Earl Parker Hanson in his book, *Transformation: The Story of Modern Puerto Rico:*

Federal officials took King in tow on his arrival in Puerto Rico and organized a motorcade which drove to all parts of the island to show the Senator how the Puerto Ricans lived and what the United States was doing to alleviate their lot. But he seemed in no way interested in slums or in reconstruction projects, or in anything else except the question of whether little boys and girls spoke English. Every time his car stopped he dove out, accosted some child on the road, and asked: "Do you speak English?" Invariably, of course, he got no answer at all; even if the child had known a few words of English, he would still have been so embarrassed, and so frightened by the august Senator, that he wouldn't have been able to say anything. At crossroad after crossroad the cars stopped to permit the Senator to pick out some child and ask his unvarying question: "Do you speak English? Answer me! Do you speak English?" At crossroad after crossroad that rather direct form of academic research brought the same negative results, with the Senator growing ever redder in the face and ever more convinced that he had the solution to the Puerto Rican problem. Then, in the southern part of the island, he came a cropper, with disastrous results to the Puerto Rican educational system.

The road crossed a river, but the water was too high for the cars to negotiate the ford. The motorcade stopped while somebody went for a yoke of oxen to pull the various cars across. While it stood there, naturally, a group of boys gathered to gawk, and the Senator had his golden opportunity. He accosted the group, but almost immediately the boys began to dance around him, shouting like Comanche Indians.

"Do you spik Eeenglish? Do you spik Eeenglish?" yelled the young rascals, who ranged in ages up to sixteen. "Do you spik Eeenglish? Do you spik Eeenglish?" With fiendish bursts of derisive laughter and impolite gestures, they danced around the Senator in unholy glee. King dove back into the car to smolder in defeat, but the insult from the youngsters was to have far-reaching results.

Senator King went back to Washington with a personal revelation of The Puerto Rican Problem. The answer was obviously to stop teaching that foreign language — Spanish — in the schools, and make everyone learn English as soon as possible.

Part of the early results of all this was an atmosphere on the island in which a Puerto Rican in the educational system who did not favor all-out English instruction was looked upon by Federal officials as anti-American and possibly subversive. On the other hand, a Puerto Rican who favored the new U.S. attitude was looked upon by his fellow islanders as something of a sell-out. Reasons for either view were not so important as the view itself. Thus, as part of the first attitude, a high school teacher name Inés Mendoza (who later became the wife of Governor Muñoz Marín) lost her job after testifying before a congressional committee that in her opinion the system of doing all the teaching in English was a bad educational method for the children of Puerto Rico.

As part of the result of the second attitude, no top Puerto Rican was willing to take on the job of Commissioner of Education on the island with the new demand from Washington for an all-out emphasis on English. Washington searched and finally found a man who was willing to take the job, along with the official Federal philosophy — a Spanish instructor in a college in Charleston. Dr. José Gallardo was appointed in 1937 and received the following letter from President Roosevelt:

I desire at this time to make clear the attitude of my administration on the extremely important matter of teaching English in Puerto Rico. Puerto Rico came under the American flag thirty-eight years ago. Nearly twenty years ago Congress extended American citizenship to Puerto Ricans. It is regrettable that today hundreds of thousands of Puerto Ricans have no knowledge of the English language. Moreover, even among those who have had the opportunity to study English in the public schools, mastery of the language is far from satisfactory. It is an indispensable part of American policy that the coming generation of American citizens in Puerto Rico grow up with complete facility in the English tongue. It is the language of our nation. Only through the acquisition of the language will Puerto Rican Americans secure a better understanding of American ideals and principles. Moreover, it is only through familiarity with our language that Puerto Ricans will be able to take full advantage of the economic opportunities which became available when they were made American citizens.

Few Puerto Ricans outside of the Nationalist party would have argued with those sentiments; the argument was rather with the means to be employed in achieving the desired end. The experience on the island had been that complete instruction in English resulted in neither a good understanding of English nor even a minimum understanding of other subjects taught by this method to Spanish-speaking children.

Dr. Gallardo experimented. A kind of compromise plan was employed whereby English was used as the language of instruction part of the time. Toward the end of Gallardo's tenure, the method was to use Spanish as the language of instruction in the first two grades, then gradually introduce English as the language of instruction until the teaching in the seventh grade was supposedly two thirds in English. This part-time English, part-time Spanish system failed to change the language pattern of the island in its first years of trial and error, and in 1943 Gallardo was reprimanded by Secretary of the Interior Harold Ickes. When Gallardo's term expired in 1945 he was beloved by neither San Juan nor Washington.

Officials both on the island and on the mainland agreed that a new Commissioner of Education ought to be appointed. The appointee, however, would have to get U.S. Senate approval, and the Senate was asking for a written guarantee of purpose in stressing the English language in the educational system. Rafael Pico, then chairman of the Puerto Rican Planning Board, was nominated for the position, and soon afterwards a news story quoted a representative of the U.S.

Department of the Interior as saying that Mr. Pico would not be considered until he "clarified" his views on teaching English. Mr. Pico wrote to Secretary Ickes asking for his name to be withdrawn. He said then:

. . . Briefly stated I believe in stressing under any political status the teaching of English in Puerto Rico as an essential subject of our curriculum. With this aim there is no controversy either here in Puerto Rico or in the States. As to the methods for reaching this goal there is, and has been a continuous controversy for at least the past twenty-five years. My contention is that the point in question is not a subject for political interference, but should rightfully be reserved for educators and experts on the methods of acquiring a second language. With all candor, I have to state that the consensus of educators familiar with the Puerto Rican problem is that the goal of better English is best achieved by stressing the teaching of English as a subject without interfering with the use of the mother tongue as the language of instruction in the other subjects of the curriculum. Although I sympathize with this point of view, as I stated in my extension of remarks, I postponed the outlining of a definite policy as to methods until I could have an opportunity to examine in the Department of Education the results obtained with the methods used by my predecessors in the Department.

Any further commitment on my part, I felt, and still feel, is unwarranted and would handicap the freedom of action that I, or any other new Commissioner of Education, should have on entering the position. Puerto Rico needs a new educational policy, not only in the question of English, but throughout all the curriculum, so that our educational system will really serve the best interest of the community, which is engaged in a far-reaching program of social and economic reform . . .

In 1948 when an act of Congress granted the Puerto Ricans the right to elect their own governor, that governor was able to appoint his own education commissioner without interference from the mainland. The man named to the job by Governor Luis Muñoz Marín was Mariano Villaronga, and under his guidance the island education system really began to grow. It had, however, not been at a standstill despite the wrangles over English teaching, and great strides had been made from the miserable conditions of 1899; with the new home-controlled government, the strides became longer and faster. By 1940, the percentage of children between six and eighteen attending school had risen from the 8 per cent of 1899 to 50 per cent. By 1957 it was up to 94 per cent in the elementary schools, 84 per cent in intermediate schools, and 43 per cent in high schools. The literacy rate moved from 15 per cent in 1899 to 68.5 per cent in 1940, to 80 per cent in 1955. Under Muñoz Marín, Puerto Rico was using a third of its total budget for public education. Expenditure of public funds for education rose from $24 per pupil annually in 1940 to $71 annually by the mid-fifties. In his report to the Third Legislature of Puerto Rico in 1957, Governor Muñoz Marín was able to report on education that "enrollment has exceeded established goals at all school levels." On the matter of language instruction, Muñoz Marín reported:

During the year, the first group of Puerto Rican English teachers was sent for instruction to the United States, to live in English-speaking communities. A difficulty encountered in the teaching of English — which is from all viewpoints so badly needed as a second language of the Puerto Ricans — is that the great majority of English teachers are people whose vernacular is not English. It is neither possible nor desirable to import thousands of teachers from the United States to replace other thousands of teachers in Puerto Rico. Nevertheless it is clear that a good English teacher must be truly familiar with the language's usage. In the years to come, more groups — more than a thousand teachers — will therefore be sent to spend a full year in United States communities where there are few other Puerto Ricans, and where they can so accustom themselves to the daily, familiar use of the language the teaching of which is their main task. Ninety were sent this year. It is planned to send two hundred or more every year. The plan deserves the legislature's full support, which, I am sure, it will receive.

The migration of teachers was, fortunately, not a one-way program. In 1955 five teachers from the U.S. mainland changed places with five teachers from Puerto Rico, and an annual exchange of fifty teachers from island and mainland was soon being planned. The program was a minor reflection of the unplanned yearly migration of students, which in 1957 was estimated at a yearly average of 5000 children who go from Puerto Rico to the mainland, and 1500 who return from the mainland to Puerto Rico.

The experience is in many ways more essential for the U.S. teachers than the Puerto Rican teachers. The Puerto Rican teachers of course learn better English and perhaps new methods of instruction. The U.S. teachers see the "minority group" students on their own home grounds and have a chance to learn something of Puerto Rican life and culture that is not conveyed in the clichés and prejudice of most information about the Puerto Ricans in New York. The experience has been an enriching one for the Puerto Rican students of the classes they return to teach.

Raymond S. Sayers, one of the first group of five U.S. main-

land teachers to take part in the exchange program, wrote a
warm and revealing account of his experience for the New
York City High School teachers' magazine, *High Points*.
Comparing his year of contact with Puerto Rican students on
the island and students in New York City, Mr. Sayers made
these observations, which destroy the mainland stereotype of
life in Puerto Rico, and by extension illuminate the failure of
schools in Spanish Harlem as a failure not of the students but
of the system.

Teaching is often a painful process in the slum school in
New York. Even when there is satisfactory discipline and
the teacher has the respect and cooperation of his class, he
is not likely to encounter much enthusiasm for his subject,
and he has to rack his brains to find ways of making watered
down material palatable to his pupils. Shakespeare is es-
chewed in the English classes, and foreign languages are
banished from the curriculum. The situation is quite different in Puerto Rico, where most secondary students attend
high schools that offer the traditional academic or commercial course. All are required to study what for them is a
very foreign and difficult language, English, and the Spanish
curriculum is heavily laden with such classic novelists as
Cervantes and Galdós and such famous dramatists as Lope de
Vega and the Duque de Rivas. Because we exchange teachers
were assigned to English classes, we were unable to judge
the students' reaction to such solid fare. However, as far as
English is concerned, we were happy to discover that the
boys and girls were very receptive learners. In addition they
were pleased — unjustifiably so — at being taught by native
speakers of English instead of their own excellent Puerto
Rican teachers. The situation is very different from that
prevailing in the United States, where foreign languages
have always vied with mathematics for the distinction of
being the most unpopular subject in the high school cur-

riculum. Not only did the boys and girls all study English, but they studied it rather well in spite of difficult home conditions, for most are members of very large families that live in small crowded cottages in which privacy is an undreamed-of luxury, and in which there is always the noise of a crying baby or a neighbor's television set.

What I have said above may suggest that the Puerto Rican school student has different interests from the American boy. Perhaps it would be more accurate to say that he has a broader range of interests. He will go to a field day in the local stadium, a senior class day at the beach, or a prom at the luxurious Caribe Hilton Hotel (for which he will have been saving for three years) and enjoy himself as much as any continental youth, but he will also respond to a poetry recital or contest in a way that the continental youth would not. Traditionally the Latin Americans have been such sincere lovers of poetry that college students almost always know strings of poems from memory and a great many try their hands at verse. In the United States an M.D. who is a fine poet as well, like William Carlos Williams, is a rare phenomenon, but there are many verse-writing physicians in Latin America, and Puerto Rico's greatest modern poet, Luis Llorens Torres, was also a distinguished and successful lawyer. A popular institution in the Latin countries is the professional poetry declaimer, who gives recitals in the theatres and on the radio and who may even be called upon to recite at dinners or public meetings. When it was announced at the Central High School in San Juan that Mario Cox, a well-known declaimer, was going to give a program in an afternoon assembly, I doubted whether there would be anyone in the audience, but the school auditorium was filled with boys and girls who listened intelligently to an excellent recital of poems in a difficult Negro dialect, by writers of the Afro-Cuban and Afro-Puerto Rican schools. I am sure that even Carl Sandburg would not have done so well in an American school.

I was more amazed at another event which took place after school one hot April day. It was a literary assembly in two parts. The first was a reading of students' prize-winning poems, which had been selected from among many submitted to the Department of Spanish, and the second part was a poetry recitation contest, in which the winner was chosen from among a group of several contestants who had survived previous eliminations. This affair, which lasted well over an hour and a half, was attended by a thousand students, and after it was over I noticed that many of them were standing about in groups, commenting on the interpretations of the poems and the judges' decisions.

In San Juan, the Puerto Rican high school boy hangs around after school to hear poetry readings. In New York City, the Puerto Rican high school boy — having adapted himself to the more advanced culture of the mainland — is more likely to be found hanging out with a gang in a candy store.

Puerto Ricans in New York who still read poems are a triumph of heritage over environment — and, more specifically, a triumph over the New York City school system. When the school system made its first recorded study of the problems of Puerto Rican students, several generations of Puerto Ricans had already passed through its grades and there were 200,000 Puerto Ricans living in the city. The year of that first study was 1947, and since then a series of studies, reports, and recommendations have been made. It was not, however, until 1958 — a little more than a decade after its first study — that the school board put into practice a uniform, city-wide program designed to meet the needs of the Puerto Rican students. By then there were 114,000 Puerto Rican students in the New York City schools.

Excerpts from the studies themselves present the best indi-

cation of the history of New York City school instruction of
the Puerto Rican students. In 1952 representatives from the
staffs of the junior high schools in East Harlem made a report
on "Education of the Non-English Speaking and Bi-lingual
(Spanish) Pupils." Among the findings of the report were the
following items from the junior highs of this district, which
had by that time (1952) been teaching Puerto Rican students
for more than thirty years:

> . . . For our children who spend their early childhood in
> Puerto Rican schools, there is no continuity of education,
> as we know very little about the curriculum of each school
> level.
>   The consensus is that standardized tests of intelligence,
> reading, and arithmetic are of little practical value to us be-
> cause they lack validity for the pupils tested. Such tests are
> based on an experiential background which is foreign to the
> children. Furthermore, most of these group intelligence
> tests are dependent on the ability to read. One school which
> has a very large non-English speaking student body has
> used the New York City tests of reading progress and tests
> of fundamental operations with some success in advanced
> groups. Most schools, however, do not have a formal testing
> program. The committee agrees that informal tests give a
> truer picture of the pupils' abilities and achievements.

Under the topic of "Health Needs":

> Many of the pupils need eyeglasses. Some need surgical
> care. One of the schools provided surgery through a legacy
> memorializing a deceased teacher . . . Some of the schools
> in the districts raise funds through the assistance of enter-
> tainers who sponsor annual shows. Funds are earmarked for
> needy Puerto Ricans. Through the Junior Red Cross and
> the cooperation of neighborhood optometrists, eyeglasses

are secured at reduced rates for a few pupils each term. We have found that eight or ten weeks elapse before the pupil gets the badly needed eyeglasses. If the eyeglasses break, sometimes months elapse before they are replaced.

Under the topic "Teaching English as a Second Language":

Each principal is doing what he believes is best for the children within the limitations set by the organization permitted by the junior high school division.

The history of teaching a second language on the island was one of "vertical anarchy"; in New York City it has been one of "horizontal anarchy." Whereas the method of instruction in Puerto Rico changed with the political winds, it at least was uniform for all the schools at any given time. In New York, until 1958, the language problem was handled by "each principal doing what he believes is best for the children within the limitations set by the organization permitted by the junior high school division." This often meant no method at all — the Puerto Rican students were merely put in classes with the other children and had to get by as best they could. It often meant the "method" described by the assistant principal of P.S. 168, in which the teachers — even those who knew some Spanish — were allowed to speak to the children only in English.

María Flores, who went through this system, and now is watching her daughters go through it, explained that in cases where the family speaks mainly Spanish at home and the teachers speak only English at school, "the first couple years are lost on the kids. It takes a couple of years before they understand English well enough to really know what's going on, and by then, of course, they've lost all the instruction they should have been getting in the other subjects in the first two years. They never really catch up."

"Never catching up" often means never learning to read and write in English.

The first active attempt by the Board of Education to cope with the language problem came in 1948, when the Substitute Auxiliary program was devised. These teachers were to be bilingual in Spanish and English. They would visit schools with a high percentage of Puerto Rican students, and in the morning meet with small groups of newly arrived children to help "orient" them to the community and teach them fundamental English. In the afternoons, they would meet with newly arrived parents. When the program was initiated in 1948, there were eight of these S.A.T. teachers for the city of New York. The number was increased to ten in 1951 and finally got its first substantial boost in 1957 when fifty more S.A.T.'s were hired, bringing the total to seventy-six for the city. For a school population including more than 100,000 Puerto Rican students, this was obviously a valuable but stopgap program, and it did not have anything to do with the regular classroom instruction.

In the classroom itself there were few bilingual teachers, and by 1958 there still were relatively few on a regular basis. The reason for this has not been lack of supply so much as lack of demand on the part of the Board of Education. The stringent, often criticized requirements of diction and accent set by the New York City school board for regular teachers makes it extremely difficult for bilingual teachers with a Spanish-speaking background to get anything but a substitute position in the school system. In 1957 the Education Division of the Commonwealth of Puerto Rico Migration Division in

New York City compiled a brochure of information on the supply of teachers of Puerto Rican origin living in the New York metropolitan area and seeking positions on the mainland. The study was made on the basis of 155 Puerto Rican teachers whose applications for employment were on file with the Commonwealth of Puerto Rico's New York office. All but three of the applicants held college degrees. There were 132 with Bachelor's degrees and twenty with Master's degrees. Eighty-eight (57 per cent) of the applicants indicated that their English was "fluent"; and fifty-eight (37 per cent) that it was "moderate." Seventy-four of the applicants attended a series of orientation conferences sponsored by the Commonwealth, and twenty-four others completed a fifteen-week English-improvement course. Out of that number a representative of the Education Division of the Commonwealth of Puerto Rico Migration Division said that in 1958 only "several" had been hired as regular teachers in the New York school system.

The need for bilingual teachers has been debated on both sides by city officials. In 1951 the subcommittee on Education, Recreation, and Parks of the Mayor's Committee on Puerto Rican Affairs made what was then the most complete study of the Puerto Rican students in the New York schools and reported the following:

> In the schools whose total school population is over 26% Puerto Rican, only 5% of the teachers claim any skill in the use of Spanish. In districts having 49% and 42% Puerto Ricans, we find that only 7.6% and 6.1% respectively of the teaching body can communicate with the pupils or their parents in a common language . . . If increased proportionately to the Puerto Rican school population, we should need

approximately 1,000 real Spanish-speaking teachers . . . Almost one third of the schools reporting have no Spanish-speaking teachers.

We disagree with the viewpoint that the teachers' use of Spanish in the classroom serves as a crutch. If we accept as our basic goal the child's adjustment to his new environment, it is important that he communicate . . . in Spanish until he is able to express himself somewhat adequately in English.

But the study whose findings were the basis of the first city-wide classroom program of instruction for the Puerto Rican students reached a different conclusion. The "Puerto Rican Study," begun in 1954 with help from Ford Foundation funds and carried on in experimental school situations in New York, listed six major points of "general agreement" in its findings. The final point was that "knowledge of Spanish is useful but is not essential to successful teaching of English to Spanish-speaking children."

The program worked out by the Puerto Rican Study is based on a series of textbooks and guides for both teachers and pupils, all of which are based on the assumption that the teacher does not know Spanish. There are some full-time bilingual teachers in the schools, though it is extremely doubtful that their number is anything near the thousand that the Mayor's Committee report saw necessary in 1951. Exactly, or even roughly, how many there are is unknown. When asked how many regular classroom teachers there were who were bilingual in Spanish and English in the school system in 1958, a Board of Education official said that "there wouldn't be any way of knowing that."

The twisted problems of instruction in the school are accompanied of course by the problems of the school building itself — it is likely to be of the old and crumbling variety. A study concentrating on the physical facilities of the schools attended mainly by Negro and Puerto Rican children in New York City was undertaken for the Board of Education in 1954. It compared "schools composed primarily of continental white children and schools populated essentially by Negro and Puerto Rican children."

Published in 1955, the report found that schools with heavy Negro and Puerto Rican attendance were on the average ten or twenty years older than other schools; that they were not as well maintained as predominantly white schools; that "if tenure, probationary, and substitute status are measures of competency," the teachers of Negro and Puerto Rican schools were less competent because fewer of them were on tenure and more had probationary or substitute status.

As far as the problem of segregation is concerned, the report found that the concentration of Negro and Puerto Rican children in certain schools was not due to any fault of the Board of Education but to the concentration of Negroes and Puerto Ricans in specific neighborhoods, which are of course specific school districts. In a fascinating "interpretation" of the report, the magazine *U.S. News and World Report* put it this way:

> These investigations criticized the Board of Education for not doing all it could to promote integration. But they concluded that segregation was not the result of Board policy. They blamed it, instead, on the tendency of Puerto Ricans and Negroes to crowd into certain neighborhoods . . .

What a lamentable tendency.

Within one of those neighborhoods — in East Harlem —

a group of parents and community leaders got together in 1955 to take some action on their own. The movement began as the result of a Town Hall meeting called by the New York City Youth Board to gather general information about the neighborhood. The Youth Board called for no further Town Hall meetings and, having assembled its own information, went on about its business. The people answered questions, the meeting was closed, and that was presumably the end of it. But the people present began to talk among themselves. Therein lay the seeds of revolt. What followed brings to mind the wise words of Dr. Dan W. Dodson, director of the Center for Human Relations and Community Studies of New York University, who remarked in a speech that "it is difficult to develop a sense of community when city agencies themselves fragment it. Sometimes one wonders if the bureaucrats do not do it on purpose in order to keep the people from organizing to demand more creative services from them."

Not only are the city services and agencies fragmented, but so are the neighborhoods that most need their help. East Harlem has no community newspaper; it has no focal point; it has no way of knowing what its neighbors a few blocks away are doing. As Mrs. Ellen Lurie, a lady who attended the Town Hall meeting, later explained about its impact, "That was the first time a lot of us had seen each other. People from different projects and different schools were there, people of Puerto Rican and Negro and Italian background, and all of us got to talking about our different problems. We decided we ought to get together more often, and maybe we could get things done that we couldn't get done by ourselves."

They did get together — and they did get things done. Ellen Lurie was, and is, right in the middle of it. Mrs. Lurie is a short, attractive, blond young lady who had worked for several years at the Union Settlement House on East 104th Street with neighborhood activities. Her energies seem equal to nothing less than the invasion of Europe, and through her work she won a special citation from the Council of Spanish Organizations of New York City and has become what might be called the Florence Nightingale of the East Harlem schools. And if any sick body needed a Florence Nightingale, it was indeed the East Harlem schools. But that appellation seems a bit tame, and it might be really more accurate to call Ellen Lurie the Mary Lease Teague of the East Harlem schools. Miss Teague was the lady of the Populist movement who uttered the immortal exhortation, "What you farmers need to do is raise less corn and more hell."

Under Ellen Lurie's leadership the people of East Harlem began, in the most proper and efficient of ways, to raise more hell and more schools. The first action is quite necessary to — and in fact, inseparable from — the second. Both became the province of the people who got together after the Town Hall meeting and formed an action group called the East Harlem Citizens Committee. Ellen became its principal guide and better schools its principal goal.

When they met the first time to "do something" about the neighborhood, they faced an assortment of challenges whose scope and depth was monumental. The problems in every area of community life, from crime to housing, work to narcotics, were painfully acute. It is an indication of the people's understanding of the trap they are living in that the problem they immediately were most concerned with was education. The subcommittee on schools became the main interest and the most active part of the Citizens Committee. In three years' time, through an endless round of studies, public hearings, visits to city officials, rallies, and campaigns, real progress was made in improving the local school facilities.

It is often the case that the schools of a slum neighborhood are given the least attention because its citizens exert the least pressure on public officials. Funds are ordinarily given to satisfy the neighborhoods with the most active and vocal community groups. The more sophisticated and prosperous citizens are much more likely to know how to "see their councilman," and use the most pressure to get the best facilities. And yet, the slum areas are usually the oldest areas of a city, with the oldest facilities, and most in need of improvements. When the East Harlem Citizens Committee made its first study of neighborhood schools in 1956, it found that of the fifteen elementary schools in the area, eight were built before the turn of the century; five were built before 1925; and only two were built after 1940 (1949 and 1951). They found that five of the junior high schools were constructed before 1928 and only two after that. The newest was built in 1943. Of all these schools, four had been "modernized" in recent years.

After three years of constant study and work, the Citizens Committee was able to report the following new look in the neighborhood school picture: construction approved on three new junior high schools and two new elementary schools, tentative completion dates of 1959 and 1960; modernization of three junior high schools and conversion of two more to co-educational facilities. The need for these new additions and improvements could be seen in the fact that in 1958, pending completion of the work mentioned above, all but two public schools in East Harlem were operating on at least a double shift of pupils, with some going in the morning and some in the afternoon. The only two schools not on a double shift were those located near uncompleted housing projects whose families had not yet been moved in. The immediate areas therefore had a temporary relief in population. When the families moved into the completed projects, the areas would of course be more heavily populated than ever before — and the schools more crowded.

In their fight for more and better schools, the people of the Citizens Committee gained their own education in the ways and workings of the city, and educated many officials with facts made eloquent by stating in simple and awful honesty the personal effects of impersonal statistics. A Puerto Rican mother from the Citizens Committee testified before a City Board of Estimate hearing that "at night our children have to sleep three and four in a bed and in the day they have to go to school in three and four shifts. How do you expect them to get an education?"

At a neighborhood meeting to discuss getting support for a new local school a father rose to say that he was not in favor of patching up the old school but rather of building a new one.

"The schools are too old here," he said. "You go through this neighborhood, you can't tell the schools from the rest of the dumps. A school should be something nice."

The problems and decisions faced by the Citizens Committee were not always so clear-cut as the question of whether or not a new school should be built. When they came to the matter of East Harlem's only high school, the citizens met a monster with many heads.

Benjamin Franklin High School was built in 1942 and its

attendance has steadily declined. The population of the neighborhood around it has steadily risen.

In New York City the junior high school graduate may apply for entrance into any high school in the city. The high schools are divided into two categories, vocational and academic. It is possible to attend an academic high school and take a vocational or business course, however, instead of the strictly academic course that prepares the student for college. In 1957 more graduates of junior highs in East Harlem went to academic rather than vocational high schools. The implication is misleading though, since a great number of these students took vocational or business courses at the academic high schools. Also the "fallout" — those who do not graduate from high school — is believed to be very high among students from East Harlem junior high schools, according to people of the Citizens Committee who have studied the matter.

Benjamin Franklin is an academic high school. In the neighborhood, however, it is more often described as an Italian high school. Located at First Avenue and 116th Street, it is in the heart of the old Italian district that is steadily giving way to Puerto Rican and Negro residents. It is also located in a spot difficult to reach except by double transportation, that is, by traveling on the Lexington Avenue subway and then transferring to a crosstown bus to First Avenue. For students who live in most of East Harlem, which mainly stretches south and west from First Avenue and 116th Street, Benjamin Franklin is hard to reach. This transportation difficulty has been cited as one of the reasons for the school's general unpopularity. But it seems to be minor to the main problem of attendance at Franklin, which hinges on its reputation as an Italian high school.

In 1942, the first year that Franklin opened its doors, the immediate neighborhood was largely Italian and so were the students of the high school. The people of the Italian community were proud of the fine new high school building and grounds — one of the few new and handsome decorations in a crumbling neighborhood — and looked on it as their own. The resentment toward the new Puerto Rican and Negro residents "taking over" the neighborhood was passed, as usual, from parents to children, and the majority Italian student group made it clear that Puerto Ricans and Negroes were not welcome at Franklin. Incidents began immediately, and stories of them grew.

Not only the high school but also the blocks around it were looked upon as Italian "territory" and Puerto Rican kids were anxious to avoid even going near the school, much less going into it. In 1957 the newspaper *El Diario* carried the story of a sixteen-year-old boy named Frank Martinez who was knifed while walking past the high school. When asked by the police if he knew who had knifed him, Martinez answered, "*Un Italiano.*" The answer was almost automatic and was no surprise to the neighborhood.

Franklin was undesirable for Puerto Ricans principally because it was dangerous. Gus, a young man of such endurance and sophistication that he went on from East Harlem's schools to get a scholarship to a midwestern college, was one of many Puerto Ricans from the neighborhood who lived fairly close to Franklin but went to Samuel Gompers High School, quite far from home. When asked once why he didn't go to Franklin, Gus looked at his questioner with some surprise and explained, as if the answer were all too obvious, "Because I'm Spanish."

Gus went on to say, however, that he once considered going to Franklin because of a rather unusual circumstance. He had an Italian friend in junior high who was going to Franklin and wanted Gus to go with him.

"This Italian friend of mine said if I went to Franklin he would speak to the guys and see that I wasn't bothered. I thought about it, but I don't know — I just didn't want the trouble."

The Puerto Rican population of Franklin has slowly and steadily risen through the years, but in nothing like the proportion of the Puerto Rican population of the blocks around it. As the Italian colony that once fed the high school steadily diminished, and the Puerto Ricans who feared the high school's reputation grew more numerous around it, the high school attendance steadily declined. The students it did get were mainly drawn from Junior High 172, which was established in the Franklin building and has constantly counseled its students to go on to Franklin high school. The junior high's attendance is dictated by zoning rules and not by choice, so Puerto Rican boys in its area had to go there. But many were still reluctant to go on to the high school. In 1957, the Italian students still were in the majority in the high school, though not in the blocks of the neighborhood around it.

When the Citizens Committee faced the Franklin problem, the suggestions ranged from abolishing the school altogether to making it a specialized high school concentrating, for instance, on science and thereby drawing students from all over the city and easing the Puerto Rican–Italian struggle. The final decision the Committee reached was the basic one that "something had to be done," but that the Board of Education should decide what would be the best course. The recommendation of the citizens was simply, as one of its members expressed it informally, that "it musn't go on as it is now."

This was the unanimous decision reached so often on so many different school problems by the Citizens Committee — "It musn't go on as it is now." At one meeting, a representative from the PTA of an East Harlem school got up to articulate the need felt and expressed so often by the Puerto Rican parents: "Our children are all several years behind in reading and way behind what the Yorkville children are doing. The schools in East Harlem have so many substitutes — one of my children this year had seven different teachers for the year! How can you settle down and learn anything with seven different teachers?"

A lady from another elementary PTA got up to add her own comment. Speaking slowly, with new and still hesitant English, she said, "It is so, our children do not know to read what they should. A child in the sixth grade, he only reads the book of the third. He should be reading the book of the sixth. It is not like this other places. It is up to us parents to do something about this. Now, we hear they are going to have it so a child who can't read the book of his grade can't go on to junior high school. It should be so. They just send them on and if they don't know to read, what good is it? It is no good."

Of the whole range and number of public schools in the East Harlem area there is only one that the parents can and do take pride in. That is P.S. 108, at 108th Street and Madison Avenue. Constructed in 1951, it is the newest school in East Harlem and one of the only two that were built in that district since 1925.

The effect of a new, nice-looking school was felt not only among the children but also by the parents and neighbors.

Out of its active PTA have come ideas and leaders that have worked to make a better community. Pedro Canino, an energetic member of the East Harlem Citizens Committee, and one of the first presidents of the new school's PTA, went on with that organization's backing to establish a local housing clinic to work for better conditions in the area.

P.S. 108 is a handsome, three-storied brick building with brightly lit classrooms and shining halls. On the wall outside of the Madison Avenue entrance an official Board of Education sign announces evening English classes for adults: "Free evening school for adults . . . Learn to speak, read, and write English . . . Program for Naturalization . . . Program for Citizenship . . ."

The sign itself is a relic of the past, its last two promises irrelevant for the Puerto Rican migrants. As citizens of the United States and travelers within its borders, they of course need not bother with "naturalization" and "citizenship" studies any more than a traveler from Texas or South Dakota. But the first sign inside the building confirms the need of the English promise of the sign outside. It reads, "*Todos que entran en este edeficio están obligados a presentarse en la oficina del Director . . .*"

El Director, the Principal, is Jack August, an enthusiastic educator who has headed P.S. 108 since its opening in 1951. Its enrollment is 94.2 per cent Puerto Rican, and it has served as one of the four experimental schools for the Board of Education's Puerto Rican Study. This has mainly meant concentration on methods of teaching language and orientation for students newly arrived from Puerto Rico.

"Every fall when school opens we get about two to three hundred new students from the island," Mr. August said.

The children are put in classes according to their facility with English. There are classes scaled from A (speaks English as well as a native) to G (speaks no English at all). Six teachers out of a staff of sixty-seven speak Spanish; the others "pick it up" in varying degrees. But speaking in Spanish is not part of the program, and Mr. August feels this is the best approach. The Puerto Rican study has provided language guides in the form of pamphlets for use by the teachers, and pantomime is also used. "In cases of words that defy dramatization," Mr. August said, "the teacher gives the word in Spanish." Each class is given a half hour every day of "intense English instruction."

The only exception to this method is in the kindergarten, where a Puerto Rican teacher speaks Spanish to the children and "brings them along" — speaking more English as the year progresses. Mr. August feels that this is an excellent help: "She does a marvelous job — gives the children a feeling of belonging."

In its orientation classes, newly arrived students are taken on trips of the neighborhood and of the city. "Before they study Germany," Jack August said, "we want them to know New York."

The students of P.S. 108 have a better opportunity to know it — and to live a useful life in it — than the children of most other schools in Spanish Harlem. But 108 has its serious handicaps despite its fine facilities and leadership. There are 1500 students in the school and it is run by necessity on three shifts — a 9-3, an 8-12, and an 11.30-3.30 shift. The children of the first, second, and third grades have only four hours of instruction a day. With an overwhelming number of them not knowing the language they are being taught in, they of course need more hours of instruction; because of overcrowding and lack of proper neighborhood school facilities, they get less hours instead.

The only new hopeful factor for the future rested in 1958 with the institution that fall of the teaching program prepared by the Puerto Rican Study. Supplemented by books and instruction guides for teachers of Puerto Rican pupils all over the city, it meant for the first time a consistent, city-wide approach to the language problem.

The Puerto Rican Study program cannot, of course, provide a cure-all. It cannot provide new buildings and new attitudes. It cannot remedy the kind of thinking expressed by one elementary school official in Spanish Harlem, who complained to a visiting Board of Education psychologist that she was unable to fill up the classes for retarded children in her school any more. She said she didn't understand it because the neighborhood, which had until recently a majority of Italian residents, used to have a "much better class of people" and in those days there were always three classes needed for the retarded children. Now the school was mainly Puerto Ricans and yet there weren't enough mentally retarded students to fill up three classes. The lady didn't think this seemed logical and wondered if perhaps the Board of Education had changed its methods of psychological testing.

Perhaps those ladies will disappear like the bad dream they are for their Puerto Rican students. Perhaps the new program provided by the Puerto Rican Study will facilitate the learning of English and revolutionize the hopeless pattern of frustration and dead-end education for Puerto Rican pupils. Perhaps the many cases of Puerto Rican men and women who were graduated from schools in Spanish Harlem without knowing how to read or write will soon become the night-mare memories of an era of adjustment — and of neglect. Even then the damage will not be undone for generations of Puerto Rican men and women who grew up in New York City's public schools with a language that was foreign to them drummed in their ears, and sat in the irony of "Opportunity classes" because they had no opportunity. Their children sit as they sat in the schools of the slums, and the terror of every slum school is intensified by the terror of an unknown language and the difficulty of grappling with it. Like the children of Stephen Spender's "Elementary School Classroom in a Slum," their faces cry out for the far-off opportunity and speak, alike, that

> *Unless, governor, teacher, inspector, visitor,*
> *This map becomes their window and these windows*
> *That open on their lives like crouching tombs*
> *Break, O break open, till they break the town*
> *And show the children to the fields and all their world*
> *Azure on their sands, to let their tongues*
> *Run naked into books, the white and green leaves open*
> *The history theirs whose language is the sun.*

The small boy stood in the flaking room of his tenement home, his eyes bright and his face eager, amidst the shambled furniture whose only new and shiny piece was a television set. "When I grow up," the boy said, "I'm going to be an airplane pilot, like the ones they have on the TV."

Sweat without Profit

. . . The first on the streets know the truth in their bones;
for these, neither Eden, nor passions unleafing;
they go to the slough of the ciphers and strictures,
to the games without genius and the sweat without profit . . .

—"Dawn" (in New York),
FEDERICO GARCÍA LORCA

THE WINTER DAWN of Harlem cleaned the streets in a bright cold luster that clarified the buildings and gave to each person a separate, definite identity that later would be lost in the dust and refuse and bustle of the lengthening day. The wind blew cold and sharp from the East River down the wide and almost deserted swath of 125th Street. At Lexington Avenue a woman with a scarf around her head and a frayed black coat whose collar was pulled up high around her neck, her hands pushed deep in the pockets, her eyes cast downward, headed past the corner drugstore toward the entrance of the soot-stained building that rose five floors above it. A young man dressed in blue slacks and a blue and gray jacket walked precisely beside her, staring not down but straight ahead. At the moment they turned the corner from Lexington onto 125th Street a dark-faced girl cried, *"Huelga! Huelga!"* (Strike! Strike!) and hurried toward them, waving a handful of leaflets. In blue and brown lettering, printed on one side in English, on the other in Spanish, was the following statement:

GET THE PROTECTION OF NEW YORK'S BIGGEST AND MOST RESPECTED UNION

As a member of the International Ladies' Garment Workers' Union, you'll get these important benefits:

— Job Security
— 35 Hour Week
— Time and a Half Overtime Pay After 7 Hours of Any Day
— Paid Holidays
— Vacation Pay
— Guaranteed Minimum Wages
— Severance Pay
— Free Medical and Hospital Care

You can help yourself — and your family — to a better life by joining the International Ladies' Garment Workers' Union.

DO IT TODAY.
IT'S THE COMMON SENSE THING TO DO.

The woman in the black coat and her young male escort ignored the plea for Common Sense without reading it. They walked faster as the woman with the leaflets approached them. A ragged chorus of jeers broke out from the dozen men and women with picket signs who marched in a slow, cold circle by the curb, opposite the building's entrance. "Scab!" came the cry, "Scab, scab!" A small man in a large overcoat, gray fedora, and maroon scarf broke from the circle of marchers and hurried along beside the couple, waving a finger at them,

scolding like a schoolteacher: "You are the shame of the Spanish people in New York!" From the entrance of the building
the manager of the Sano garment shop, which occupies the
fifth floor, jerked his head up and down and urged the couple
toward him like a track coach urging his athletes down the
last lap to the finish line. As the couple reached the entrance
a policeman stepped out — for the moment a uniformed door-
man — and let them in. They entered with the boss, amidst
rising jeers, and several moments later the young man in the
blue and gray jacket came back out to go find another woman
who was waiting for convoy. The dark-faced girl with the
leaflets walked slowly back to the corner, saying almost to herself in a low, hurt voice, "*Huelga*," and folded her arms for
warmth.

These morning rituals had been going on for five weeks in
the attempt of the ILGWU to organize the three garment
shops — Sano, Reggie, and Zaraya — in the building on the
corner. As in similar cases it was mainly a war of nerves being
waged, with the girls growing anxious over getting into
trouble with the union people outside who jeered them and
the bosses inside who promised, cajoled, and threatened them.
Many girls had drifted off to other shops or found "homework" to take in, and signs in the windows of the building on
the corner said, "Operators Needed — *Se Necesitan Opera-
rios*." A secondary war of nerves had begun inside, with the
bosses of the shops on the different floors trying to lure the
girls from other shops to their own floor once they got in the
building. The bosses who stood at the doorway had to see
their operators not only safely past the picket line, but also
safely past the doors of the rival employers within the building. The Sano boss, on the fifth floor, was most harassed, since

his workers had to pass by two temptations on the way up.

But despite these "cold war" gains, the union had not been able to recruit and hold any regular worker from the shops until this day which marked the strike's fifth week. It was later that afternoon that a woman from the Sano shop who had taken one of the union leaflets called up the ILG's Harlem headquarters to ask some questions. Mrs. Carlotta Rodríguez, who works in the Harlem office as a secretary, had taken the woman's name and made an appointment to visit her home that night. The next day, Mrs. Rodríguez told the Harlem district manager that the first real break might have come. Carlotta Rodríguez, a handsome woman with graying hair, dressed in a smart tailored suit, was beaming with the new information when she came to work.

"This lady who called has worked at Sano a long time," she said, "and she's a very nice, intelligent lady. I went to see her at her home last night — a beautiful home she has, in the projects, and three beautiful children — and I said, 'I am surprised. A lady like you, with this beautiful home and these beautiful children, and working in a place like Sano. You can do so much better in a union and have so much more time for your children. Why, you can't afford not to join. You know, every time you have a child you get $150 for the doctor bills and the time off — it *pays* you to have a child!'

"Well, she said she hadn't known. She had heard all kinds of things about the union and she said, frankly, she also had a bad impression from the picket line, with all those people yelling things at her. But she said, 'Now that you come in my home, and I see you are a nice person, I feel quite different.' She began to talk about how things were there, and oh, I had to shake my head. They give them 35¢ for every garment, no matter how hard it is, or what it is. The most she ever made was one week she made $70. You know how? Working seven o'clock in the morning to seven o'clock at night, six days a week. The girls go in at all hours — some of them we never see. We don't get there with the picket line till six o'clock, but some of the girls go in at 5.30."

The seventy-two hour week, at less than a dollar an hour, sounds like a tale of life in the New York sweatshops of thirty years ago. To the lady at the Sano garment shop, it was not a remote fact of history but a fact of life in Spanish Harlem in 1958.

The facts are well known of the poverty of the island home that most of the people of Spanish Harlem have come from; the facts are not so widely accepted of the poverty that they and their children find on their new island home of Manhattan. The scuttlebutt of bars and taxi drivers is that "the Puerto Ricans come to New York to go on relief." But when Ricardo Sanchez boarded the plane at San Juan airport and said that "it is no good to be poor," he had not put all his hopes and savings in airplane tickets with the aim of substituting one form of poverty for another. The story of Puerto Ricans on relief is largely the story of Providencia and her seven children, not living off the fat of the taxpayer's land but off the fat that comes in jars from the hospital to substitute for proper food. It is largely the story of women and children deserted by the husband and father through death or divorce, and having no possibility of income. In an average year of good employment in New York City, in 1953, a total of 5 per cent of the Puerto Rican population was unemployed, and of that number more than three fourths were women with dependent children. Welfare Commissioner Henry L. McCarthy has been quoted repeatedly as saying that the Puerto Ricans who have to go on relief get off the rolls faster than any other group of people. Many who are on relief receive what is called "supplementary relief," which means that some member of the family is holding down a job but doesn't make enough money from it to support the family. With so many large Puerto Rican families, often including a half dozen children, and with the low pay that most Puerto Ricans receive for work in New York City, the situation is inescapable.

The poverty of Spanish Harlem is especially tragic because it is a self-perpetuating poverty. The alumni of "opportunity" classes are equipped to receive no opportunity, even if they find it. Of all the members of the Conservatives Club, which represents a fairly typical bunch of boys and girls in the neighborhood, only one is even prepared for a trade. Willie Leon, for whatever obvious motivation, always had an avid interest in food. While still in junior high school he expressed a desire to go on to a vocational high school where he could learn to become a baker, and now he is learning the skills of that trade. He is alone among his comrades in facing the world after graduation with a clear opportunity to make a decent living. Most of the kids in the club don't have enough basic skills in English to qualify them for anything beyond the labor of their fathers. And yet, they are mostly of average intelligence, and many are obviously above the average. These, the ones of high I.Q. and high ambitions — ambitions, that is, above the sweat of routine labor, ambitions of escaping the slums they live in — are the ones who are often most likely to turn to crime and narcotics. One of the sharpest minds of the neighborhood belongs to Boppo Cruz, the pusher, who found in heroin the first and only visible means of escape from his surroundings and outlet for the energy and imagination that burned within him. And Boppo is not alone.

For those who turn to routine labor, there is not much opportunity even in that kind of work in Spanish Harlem. Although Puerto Ricans run small *bodegas, botánicas,* and bars in the neighborhood, the shops of *La Marqueta,* and the streets and avenues surrounding it, and practically all of the larger stores are run by Jews and Italians who were in the area before. They still hold on to their businesses and make their money, if not their home, in the slums of East Harlem. Most of the Puerto Ricans who live there must go outside of it to get a job. There are Puerto Ricans in just about every type of labor in the city, especially in the small garment, jewelry, and plastic manufacturing shops, and in the hotel and restaurant services. It is a sad indication of the difficulty with which they have been accepted into even these types of work that a shiny booklet put out by the Commonwealth of Puerto Rico found it necessary to justify their presence there. The booklet, called *The Jobs We Do,* states that the Waldorf Astoria hotel employs about five hundred Puerto Rican men and women and that the hotel management "rates them equal to the hotel's other employees in cleanliness, productivity, and punctuality." The manager of the Waldorf went the Commonwealth booklet one better on Edward R. Murrow's television show about the Puerto Ricans in 1957. The Waldorf manager said that the Puerto Ricans he employed were especially good workers because they came from a tropical climate and therefore found it easy to work in the steam and heat of the kitchens. The Waldorf — and who would have guessed it — performs a kind of public service for Puerto Ricans who can leave their cold apartments in the slums and come to the underground kitchens of the great hotel to work in the heat of home. There are no cases on record of a Puerto Rican worker mistaking the Waldorf kitchen for the beach at San Juan, but this may be due only to a lack of imagination in tropical peoples.

In Spanish Harlem there are no great hotels, and the people who work in the neighborhood perhaps come closer to memories of home with the farmed-out needlework of garment shops than they could from the steam of the Waldorf kitchen. Needlework has long been a widely practiced skill on the island, and the small, often fly-by-night dress shops in Spanish Harlem constitute the main chance for employment within the neighborhood. It is nearly all women's work, and very few girls grow up in these streets without getting a touch of it. María Flores, though now a secretary, had her share as a child, and her sister Rosie, as well as her mother, still are at work on the sewing machines.

When María and Rosie were still in grade school they worked part-time making pop-in beads for 10¢ a string, and during one summer vacation made frames for glasses in a small plastics manufacturing shop for $20 a week. Sometimes their mother, who was working in a garment shop, brought home piecework for them. María — always the family rebel — didn't like the sewing business and was glad to get an office job as soon as she could. But Rosie took to sewing right away and works today in a textile shop several blocks from her apartment on 110th Street. Rosie is a quiet, dark-haired girl of pale and perfect complexion, and large brown eyes that have the beauty, if not the fire, of her sister María's eyes. When she and María talk about their jobs it is Rosie who speaks with a steady detachment, and sometimes warmth, of the work she does. María's voice often is shaken with anger and disgust at the work she had to do, and it rises not in warmth but in pride in speaking of the office work she does now. As for Rosie — she tried office work and didn't like it:

"María likes it fine, but I never did. I worked in two or three offices, filing and making phone calls, but it all just bored me. To me, the sewing machine is a challenge — each new garment is a challenge. There's a way to do it fast and a way to do it right. I took to it right from the start. Mother used to bring me home belts and blouses — simple things at first — and I worked them right here at the machine at home. My mother and my aunt both helped me, and I got real good. But I tell you, not right away. They have these 'schools' you know that are supposed to teach you to be an operator in a week. You pay them all right, but I tell you in a week all you can do is learn how to run the machine. Mother first brought things home for me when I was eleven, and it wasn't till I was sixteen that I was ready to go out in a shop.

"I've worked in a lot of them around the neighborhood, and the one where I am now is the best. I tell you, you don't find many like this one. Well lighted, and clean, and nice machines — they're even painted nice colors. In summer we've got four big fans going, and it's as nice a place as you could find. There's a fire escape right by the window, too, and it lowers down to the street real quick so we all could get out. One place I was in at 107th Street, you didn't have any fire escape and the building was a wreck. If it ever caught fire we'd have all been gone. Once I know the fire inspector came around and he said to the manager, 'What have you been doing, slipping some dollars to the firemen around here?' He said the boiler in the building was held together by a hairpin. But this place I'm in now — Mr. Post, he owns the place — has the boiler checked all the time. You see, when the flames turn yellow instead of blue it means the boiler's getting clogged up and is dangerous. Well, Mr. Post checks that boiler every week and if it even begins to get yellow flames he has it cleaned out. And we've got that fire escape too. Mom's right next to it. She'd be the first one out the window.

"Mr. Post is wonderful to work for — not like most of them. He calls us 'his girls.' He's not Spanish, but he's very nice to us. Sometimes on Saturdays when some of us drop by or when he sees us in the neighborhood he buys us lunch, anything we want. I've been working for him a long time, and he even knows me by name. There's so many girls — there's seventy of us — a lot of us don't even know each other by name. We all have a number — each machine has a number — and we go by the number. Most of the girls have names alike anyway. Everybody's Rosie and Carmen and Connie and Anna, and we just go by number to tell us apart. I'm Number Thirty-three. Mom's Number Five. You call in to say you're sick and give your name and nobody knows you. You say you're Number Thirty-three and they say, 'Oh, that's too bad, we'll tell Mr. Post. Hope you get better now.'

"Mom and I both are in the union now — that's the International Ladies' Garment Workers' Union — and we get sick pay and holidays and all that. I tell you it's such a difference too. We even get paid when we have a baby — $150 for the time off and doctors' bills! And such a difference in the work, too. Not just getting paid more, but more relaxed. In the shops that don't have a union it's always a fight to get your work. I've worked those too, and you have to get there early in the morning and grab for the work. You come at eight or nine o'clock on a slow day and it's all gone and you just go

home. And then you're working fast as you can to get done
even if you make it so you get the next batch. In our shops we
divide it up, so whatever work there is for the day, we all have
some. And then we get a minimum of $42.50 a week no mat-
ter what, but most of the time it's lots more, usually $70 or
$80. The union makes a lot of difference, and all the girls go
to meetings too. We're glad to belong."

Rosie is lucky and glad of her luck. There are still many
women in Spanish Harlem who work in shops that are still
unorganized — and often unknown — by the union. The
ILGWU estimates that there are thirty-five steadily operating
garment shops in East Harlem and twenty-five of that number
are organized. But many shops, like the one on East 100th
Street without a sign or a window, are known only to the
women who work there in dirty and dark conditions. There
are also shops which give out "homework" for substandard
fees, and are almost impossible to trace for their source of supply. Sometimes the small, fly-by-night shops are too precarious in operation for the union even to approach them. They
work on such a small margin of survival that unionization and
standard wages and conditions would put them out of their
threadbare business.

The shops unknown or unorganized by unions have a whole
world of devices to hold their workers at the lowest and
cheapest conditions. These methods of course are much
easier to use on workers who don't know the language and
laws of the city, and the managers press that advantage to the
hilt. A shop that opened on 106th Street promised new
workers a guaranteed wage of $42 a week and paid them all
$29 each at the end of the week. When the girls asked where
the other thirteen dollars was, the boss said that had been

"taken out for taxes." It seemed but another of the city's tragic mysteries.

Most of the non-union shops pay the sewing machine operators a flat rate of 35¢ for every garment they finish, no matter how difficult the garment is to make, or how long it takes. The unions, which also work by the piece, have a set scale determined by the contract that rates each garment according to the difficulty of the work, and many of the garments that a union operator makes for 70¢ or 90¢ still get only 35¢ in the non-union shop. But it is part of the method of the sweatshop boss to pay a few of the girls much more highly than the others. There are always a few women who complain and threaten to quit or call in a union. The boss will draw these ladies aside and secretly raise their scale much higher, sometimes double the rate of the other workers. These women then stay quiet and help the boss keep the other workers in line.

The boss also has his own devices for insuring the quiet and uncomplaining work of the other women. Since most of the people who work in such shops have little cash on hand at any time, they furnish their homes and families' needs with installment buying. A credit reference is usually needed, and the boss of the sweatshop is only too glad to provide it. He may even loan the women five or ten dollars to help them make the first payment. Then, when the time finally comes, as it did on 125th Street, that a union starts to picket and try to recruit, the boss tells the women that if they join the union or leave the shop he will call the furniture store or the clothing store where he has given his name as a reference and have everything that the woman is paying installments on taken away from her. This often means the entire furnishings of a home. The women are seldom anxious to test the challenge.

The boss of the sweatshop is usually a personnel man of the highest skill. He judges each woman and in his role as lord and supplier of income gives and takes away at the proper psychological moments. When a woman takes a vacation after several years, the boss will often pat her on the back, wish her a happy trip, and slip her a five-dollar bill. That is vacation pay, gratis, out of the boss's good will and generosity. Anytime the workers need ready cash the boss is ready to supply it. He knows he will get it back and more, and the more the worker is in his debt the stronger is the boss's hold on her.

Against these time-tested systems of command the unions must wage the kind of slow, hard battle that the ILG was putting up against the shops on 125th Street. But it is not just the boss's opposition that makes things difficult. It is also the bitter distrust and hostility of thousands of Puerto Rican workers in New York who regard the unions not as a liberating force but as another agent of exploitation.

The antipathy of Puerto Ricans to unions is not a sentiment that migrants carry with them when they come to New York. The labor movement in Puerto Rico has a long and honorable, if largely ineffectual, history. From the later years of the nineteenth century, when Santiago Iglesias, the Samuel Gompers of the Puerto Ricans, was trying to organize workers on the island, the unions there were, until very recently, mostly small, independent locals that supported themselves by passing the hat. The first real change to a stronger movement began with the start of Puerto Rico's "Operation Bootstrap" in 1940, which lured mainland industry with the promise of cheap labor and a ten-year tax exemption. When mainland industries began to move to the island in growing numbers, mainland labor unions soon began to follow. By 1958 there were ten in-

ternational unions operating locals on the island, but they had
been able to organize only twenty-seven of the 455 new
"Bootstrap" factories. They faced an extremely difficult challenge, for the advanced labor laws of Puerto Rico provide for
the sort of security that was gained on the mainland through
union collective bargaining. Puerto Rico has a workman's
compensation act that applies to every business on the island
with three or more employees, no matter what the wage level
may be; a maternity welfare law that guarantees time off and
half-pay four weeks before and four weeks after childbirth;
workers in nonseasonal jobs are entitled to one month's severance pay if laid off without just cause. Wages too are largely
determined by government action. Minimum-wage committees composed of representatives from management, labor, and
government set the minimum legal pay rates for different
types of work within each industry.

The international unions actually spend great effort and are
very effective in increasing wage rates at the committee hearings. But since the union's role in the hearings is to press for
as high a rate as the industry can bear, they are unable to go
much higher when it comes to their own collective bargaining
with companies of that industry. The direct benefits they are
able to offer to the workers as reward for paying dues and
initiation fees are necessarily small. The real bargaining table
in Puerto Rico is the minimum-wage board hearing, and the
unorganized worker benefits just as much as the union man.

The contact of workers with organized labor on the island
has been a limited one, but a happy one. It is in New York
that the Puerto Ricans have learned a bitter contempt for
unions.

It was not until the fall of 1956 that the story of the thousands of Puerto Ricans trapped in racket unions in New York City came to light. It was not until then that the Puerto Rican workers happened to find an organization that was able and willing to help them. In the fall of that year a group of Puerto Rican workers brought a letter to a private organization in the city known as the Association of Catholic Trade Unionists. The workers asked that the letter be sent to the proper authorities. It read, in unaltered text, as follows:

New York City, October 29, 1956
American Federation of Labor

Dear Sir,
    We, the employes of the Starke Design Co. are writting this letter to call your attention about this problem. We belong to local union No. 122, I.J.W.U., and we are not in according with the agreement of this union.
    We have to pay $3 monthly dues and we don't know the benefits we derive from this.
    We want somebody come to investigate this. If not come in this week.
    Thanks for the attention to this letter.
                                    EMPLOYES OF STARKE DESIGN CO.

The letter was signed by forty-nine Puerto Rican workers. Within a month, all of them were fired.

This was only one in a flood of cases of a new type of union-management cooperation that was taking place throughout the city. In impressive numbers, leaders of racket unions and employers had joined together in a common cause: exploitation of the Puerto Rican workers.

The first case that was brought to the attention of the ACTU was in many ways typical of what was to come. In March of 1955, Local 1648 of the Retail Clerks International

Association, AFL-CIO, signed a "backdoor" contract — that is, a contract made by the union leader and employer without the knowledge of the workers — with Morgan's Leather Goods and Rudee's Leather Goods of New York City. The workers first learned that they were members of a union in April of 1955 when the bosses at Morgan's and Rudee's called them in to give them the choice of joining the union picked by the employers or losing their jobs. Under this pressure, the workers signed membership cards and had $4 a month taken out of their pay for dues. The average weekly pay of the workers was $42. Two workers who asked the union to let them see the contract were fired by their boss. In August of 1956, the workers of the Morgan and Rudee shops formed their own union, the Workers Organizing Committee, and petitioned the National Labor Relations Board for an election on October 2. The employers and the union leaders held a meeting of the workers and told them they would have to pay dues to Local 1648 or be fired. The workers began to picket the shop on October 3 and the employers brought suit to enjoin the pickets. Lawyers provided by the ACTU represented the workers before the New York State Supreme Court and the suit was dismissed. The strike was broken, however, when employees of the New York City Welfare Department took new workers through the picket lines.

This story was published in *El Diario* and from then on complaints of Puerto Rican workers began flooding into the office of the ACTU. The ACTU began to compile a record of the cases they handled, and after six months found the following things in common with most of the complaints that came to them: contracts never seen by the workers; pay average of $40-42 a week with a general high of $45; no union meetings; no union elections; no grievances processed by the union; lay-offs of workers just before they were due to get vacation or holiday periods with pay; seldom any seniority; seldom any welfare or sickness benefits; workers signed up in the union under threat of firing by the boss.

The practice of employers and racket unions working together to establish these conditions had become such an institution that it had even developed its own terminology. A Puerto Rican who had worked as an organizer for several unions in New York City once explained a few of the most important terms of the trade — the "black and white" or "sweetheart" contract, and the "milk date." A "black and white" or "sweetheart" contract is one that provides no clauses for wages above the legal minimum wage, no provisions for sick pay, no provisions for rest periods, no provisions for seniority, and in general the minimum benefits that the employer can give the worker and still keep him working. The "milk date" is the day the contract runs out and the union leaders return to the boss to extract (milk) a fee from him for continuance of the contract, which protects the boss against the possibility of demands from the workers.

The unions that were running these operations of extraction from their Puerto Rican members represented a small minority of the unions in New York City, but they were the ones who had eagerly sought out the strangers from Puerto Rico for recruitment, knowing that workers who didn't know the language and laws of the mainland would be much easier to swindle. Local 122 of the International Jewelry Workers Union, Local 229 of the United Textile Workers, Local 679 of the AFL Pulp, Paper, and Sulphite Workers, and Local 1648 of the Retail Clerks were among the unions most often cited in complaints that Puerto Rican workers brought to the ACTU. These were not New York's largest or most powerful unions, but they came to represent "unions" in general for the estimated 100,000 Puerto Ricans who were trapped within their strangling grasp, and the grasp of others like them. Most of them were infested with leaders who had previous records of crime and petty racketeering.

As complaints against this type of union began increasing, the Commonwealth of Puerto Rico's Department of Migration called upon the city's honest unions for help. The Migration Department does the major job of helping Puerto Rican migrants find jobs, housing, and assistance on the mainland, but it was powerless to take up the tangled fight against unions that, despite their activities of exploitation, were members of the AFL-CIO. The city's large and honest unions responded by setting up an AFL-CIO Advisory Committee on Puerto Rican Affairs in 1955, but it too proved largely ineffectual. The honest unions felt themselves bound by the labor movement's no-raiding agreements, and would not do anything to help the workers who were trapped as members of racket unions.

It was not until the ACTU, after nearly a year of fighting such cases with its staff of young volunteer workers and lawyers, was called to testify before the McClellan Committee in the summer of 1957 that the labor movement really moved to straighten out the mess of exploitation of Puerto Rican workers in New York racket unions. AFL-CIO president George Meany sent a special representative to New York City to help clean up the situation, and many of the worst leaders and locals were expelled. After the action of the AFL-CIO, the worst of the mess of union-management exploitation of Puerto

Ricans was cleaned up to standard conditions. But the 100,-000 Puerto Rican workers who lived beneath those conditions for years had come to equate unions with exploitation, and the general resentment to unions within the Puerto Rican community was still a deep-rooted sentiment.

Sadly enough, thousands of Puerto Rican members of "respectable" unions have a similar feeling, which has grown out of misunderstandings and indifference on the part of union officials who understand neither the language nor the problems of the new Spanish-speaking members. There are drastically few Puerto Ricans employed by New York unions as organizers or officials, and many well-intentioned union staff people merely aren't equipped by language or experience to deal with the Puerto Rican newcomers.

The district manager for Harlem of the International Ladies' Garment Workers' Union is a dedicated man named Joseph Piscitello, who came to East Harlem with his parents from Italy before the turn of the century. At the time of the strike against the three garment shops on East 125th Street in 1958, Joe Piscitello had six months before retirement at the age of sixty-five after a quarter of a century's work with the union. Joe is a short — about five feet one — balding, silver-haired man, his face creased and weather-beaten, his blue eyes flashing as if they had a life of their own untouched by the life of the aging body. He wears a brown, single-breasted suit with a maroon, white-figured tie, looped by a gold chain clasp with the initials J.P. hanging in black and gold below it. On his left hand is a black and gold ring, circling one of the knobby fingers.

Joe Piscitello quit school at the age of twelve and went to work in the old Harlem market, now long gone, for $1.50 a week. At the age of fifteen he got a job in a garment shop where he worked seventy hours a week for a salary of $2.50. In 1909 he went on strike for the first time, and he began to find his friends and his life among the men who talked better wages, better conditions, and a better world. He met a German anarchist who worked in the grocery store on 102nd and 2nd Avenue, and from him heard about men like the anarchist Alexander Berkman, the socialist Eugene Debs, and the Italian-American syndicalist Carlo Tresca. Later he got to meet those idols. He went to the Rand School and hung around Union Square for the great debates, and continued to think of better things while he worked in a garment shop. He joined the famous "Italian" local of the International Ladies' Garment Workers' and in 1933 was an organizer for Harlem in the great ILG strike of that year. Ever since he has headed the Harlem office of the ILG. He was able to do a good job because the people in the neighborhood knew and respected him, and he spoke their language. Joe figures that then the majority of the workers of the garment shops in his area were Italians, with a few Puerto Ricans. He figures that now the majority are Puerto Ricans, with a few Italians.

During the time of the ILG strike on 125th Street, a visiting reporter had made an appointment to see Mrs. Carlotta Rodríguez at the Harlem office. It was Joe Piscitello, however, who met the visitor and ushered him in to a desk in the front office, past the desk of Mrs. Rodríguez, to say that he could probably help with any information. The office was small, and its two desks were occupied by Mrs. Rodríguez and a young Puerto Rican girl in a blue skirt and sweater. A small table and several chairs made up the only other furniture. The only decorations were four fading pictures of the great strike of '33 that hung in a row on the east wall.

The visitor asked Joe about the general conditions of the area and its specific problems of organizing. Joe crossed his legs, leaned forward, and began, in often strained and halting English, to sum up the situation.

"There are thirty-five shops in our area, and all but a few are between 104th and 125th Streets. We have twenty-five of them organized. The other ten we're working on all the time. When I came in here, in 1933, we had sixty-one shops. A lot of them have moved to Pennsylvania, New Jersey — they couldn't take the standards here; others folded up. I'd say in those days we had about 2200 members in this area, but today we have about half of that. Most of them are Puerto Ricans. That is a problem, you see, because they can't understand English, a lot of them, and we can't make them understand about the things they should have and why they should have a union. It was different in '33. The people flooded to us. We called a strike and they came like an avalanche. We had no problem with the people.

"But you see, the Puerto Ricans, they don't have the education that we have. They're doing a good job down there now, I've been a couple of weeks in Puerto Rico, but they're where we were thirty years ago with education and so on. They're just not educated you see, except for some elite like Miss Rodríguez here. But mostly they're backward. Now, when people are backward you gotta come down to their level to explain. As a rule Spanish people are distrustful of you. They've been kicked around a lot. So you gotta be nice to 'em, make 'em feel you're one of them. Some people talk about the Goddamned Puerto Ricans and that kind of language but you see, you shouldn't do that. That's not the way to do it. You don't get any results that way. You have to be *human* with them."

Joe was asked if the fact that he didn't speak Spanish made it difficult for him to organize — or if there were regular Spanish-speaking organizers for this area.

"When I speak to the workers," Joe said, "I speak in English, just like I'm speaking now, but you see, I feel, because of my *experience*, I can get across to them things that, say, another person couldn't. You see, I've worked in these shops myself, just like they do. When I have to, I have one of the girls to translate. There's usually one of the girls there who can translate for you. If there's not, if there's something to be explained, I can always call up Miss Rodríguez here and have her come over. And then for a real meeting with complicated things I can call up Saby Nehema at the main office, he's our Spanish-speaking organizer. If I call a day in advance I can get him to come up and be at a meeting."

After a while, Joe showed his visitor back to his own office. They left the front office and passed through the meeting room, which was barren except for folding chairs and additional pictures of the strike of '33. The room at the back was neat and quiet. A large desk and a large bookcase behind it were brightened by the afternoon's last wash of sunlight that poured in the single high window and striped the dark green leaves of the potted plants that were set on the sill. Joe Piscitello was smiling now, his face creased and wrinkled, his shoulders back, and his body straight, seeming to expand within this room. He walked to the desk where a picture of a bearded distinguished gentleman looked up from beneath the glass top. Joe touched a finger to the picture with pride and said, "That's Carlo Tresca — he was a friend of mine."

A photographer from a New York daily news-paper came to East 100th Street with an assignment to get a picture of "the children playing in the gar-bage." It was Sunday morning, and the children were scrubbed and dressed in their finest clothes — the smallest boys in suits and ties like their fathers', the girls in starched and lacy dresses with bright-colored bows. None were playing in the garbage. The photographer went to a storefront church on the block and asked the minister to help him carry out his assignment. The minister explained that it was Sunday, and the children didn't play in the gar-bage. The photographer, getting anxious now, said, "Look — there's some kids — over there." He ran to a garbage can, yanked off the lid, and motioned to the silent, staring children. "Hey kids — c'mere — over here! Let's play . . ."

ༀༀༀ

Orientation

Stanley H. Lowell, assistant to Mayor Robert F. Wagner and the acting chairman of the New York delegation, said that the difficulties of Puerto Rican migrants would be lessened if they gained more knowledge of mainland customs and history.

— Report on the Third Puerto Rican Migration Conference, *The New York Times,* January 21, 1958

THERE IS a sign above a basement window on East 108th Street that says "Civic Orientation Center." The window is covered by a large dark curtain, and the light behind it from the room inside serves notice that the place is open, but doesn't illuminate the thin iron steps leading down from the street level to the basement door. The steps themselves are almost invisible in the pitch-dark of the building's lower depths, and it is necessary to walk down slowly and carefully. If it is Monday night or Thursday night, from eight o'clock to around eleven, a knock at the door will bring a quick response and an opening into the clinic.

The Civic Orientation Center began as a clinic for people in the neighborhood with problems in matters of rent and housing, but its work soon broadened into other areas. It holds bazaars and fund drives to raise money for local children's activities, and part of the proceeds sponsors a Boy Scout and a Girl Scout troop and sends a number of kids to camp every summer. The Monday and Thursday night clinics became a place of help and advice for people with not only problems of rent and housing but also problems of welfare, employment, taxes, travel, installment payments, and life in general. People who spoke only Spanish were much less reluctant to take these burdens before their neighbors at the local clinic than they were to go for help from strangers at the outside agencies.

The idea and impetus of the neighborhood clinic came from the enthusiasm born of the newly built P.S. 108 and its active Parent-Teacher Association. It has been developed and carried on by Pedro Canino, former president of the PTA at P.S. 108, long-time leading citizen of Spanish Harlem, and, almost as an afterthought, employee of the local post office. Pete Canino is sometimes referred to, without protest from himself, as the "Mayor of El Barrio." The appellation has spread so far that a picture of Mr. Canino speaking with a lavishly endowed blond actress at a fund-raising dinner was published in a southern racist paper as proof of the moral degradation of New York (Canino is a man of rich brown complexion) above cutlines reporting that the lady was talking with "the unofficial Mayor of Harlem."

The racist editors would probably have been more soothed by a shot of the basement room that Canino more often inhabits of an evening. It is dingy and cold, and there are very seldom any white people, much less glamorous blond starlets, found within its walls. Two fluorescent bars of light that occasionally flicker into doubtful winks and a single bare globe at the front of the room provide the illumination. A twisted strand of flypaper dangles from the globe. The walls are papered in a fading green interspersed with a pattern of pale gray clusters that might have once represented sprays of flowers. The only decorations are a calendar, a yellowing newspaper clipping that lists the places in the neighborhood for voting registration, and a black-framed certificate of incorporation of the Civic Orientation Center. It is often said that whenever more than two Americans get together they form a committee; it seems that whenever more than two get together in Spanish Harlem they have themselves incorporated. In the Manhattan Seneca Social Club as well as the Civic Orientation Center, and in fact in almost every group in the neighborhood that owns any wall space, the certificate of incorporation occupies a central, proud position.

A little after eight o'clock one cold midwinter Monday night, the Civic Orientation Center was open for business and waiting for Canino. Several of his voluntary staff assistants were there before him — a small, large-eyed, pudgy girl of about fourteen bundled up in a parka coat and blue knee socks, sitting at a long table with several magazines spread on it dentist-office style; and a man wearing wool khaki pants, a brown sport coat, black vest, and a hat that sat jauntily on the back of his head. The man moved around the room with authority, opening the large file cabinet at the back to search out folders, going to the front to answer the door, stopping off to chat with the dozen citizens who had already assembled on the folding chairs provided for them along the room's west wall. They were mostly women, but among them were one thin young man in a leather jacket and a tall handsome fellow dressed in a stylish overcoat, a blue three-button suit, and pointed shoes of a bright orange-yellow. The women all wore their coats and scarves; the basement room was not sufficiently warmer than the weather of the street to warrant removing outdoor clothes. The citizens sat quietly, occasionally talking among themselves, most of them staring ahead at the opposite wall. Into this scene of subdued silence, about twenty minutes after eight o'clock, burst the figure of Pedro Canino. The waiting was over.

Canino entered with a stream of talk, wrenching off his overcoat, throwing it over the chair of one of the two desks at the back of the room, and pointing to the other desk for the lawyer with briefcase who trailed in his wake.

"Abuses!" said Pedro Canino, throwing up his hands, then extending them toward the waiting citizens.

"The abuses you people must endure. A crime! A shame!"

Several of the women began to giggle; a few others smiled and nudged one another. Canino, a dark-haired, broad-shouldered man, impeccably dressed in a brown suit, brown suede shoes, white shirt, and maroon bow tie with tiny white polka dots, adjusted a pair of horn-rimmed glasses on his face with the hurried yet responsible air with which a judge might put on his robes for the court. He then opened a drawer of the large green filing cabinet, pulled out a can of roach spray and, with some flourish, began to squirt the walls and the floor at the back of the room. The spraying was done rather haphazardly, the mist disappearing in the air rather than against the walls or the floor itself. The whole performance seemed more ceremony than necessity — an incantation against *las cucarachas*, those living, crawling symbols of the miserable, crumbling slum apartments that most of the people of Spanish Harlem must call home. During the spraying, Canino spoke aloud, partly in English, partly in Spanish.

"Yes, today the Mayor called me, called me right at my place of work. I had called him in the morning, but I didn't really expect *him* to call me back. But that's what he did. He is on his way to the migration conference in San Juan, but he said as soon as he got back he wanted me to come up to City Hall and sit down with him. 'Canino,' he said, 'you've got to come down to City Hall and sit down with me.' So you see, we're going to get to these abuses. Mayor Wagner wants to hear about them."

Replacing the can of spray, Canino turned to the citizens and wagged a finger at them.

"And believe me, he will *hear*."

A giggle broke out from the ladies in waiting, and Canino sat down at his desk with a stern glance in their direction. The lawyer — a tall, pale gentleman from Brooklyn with thinning yellow hair and an aura about him that suggested the possibility of his soon becoming threadbare — had seated himself at the other desk and was already busy with the first "case." His services to the Civic Orientation Center were of course free but offered the possibility of meeting prospective clients with negligence cases that might provide nice sums. Service for the lawyer in such a "clinic" amounts, more or less, to his taking pot luck. The first citizen seeking his counsel was the sharply dressed man in the orange pointed shoes. The man, it seemed, had signed up to buy a large, deluxe television set on time and had not understood the terms of the payment, which included a high interest rate he couldn't afford. Now he wanted to get out of the deal. The man did not speak English very well, and Canino looked up from some considerable shuffling among the papers in his desk to get the story. He heard it, took off his glasses, and slapped his forehead.

"When will we learn?" he asked, rhetorically.

He looked up and pointed his glasses at the people.

"*Don't* buy on down payments — do without! Wait to buy till you have the cash!"

Canino slapped the table furiously, shouting, "Don't let those leeches prey upon you!"

Readjusting his glasses, Canino called forth a woman from the folding chairs who took a seat by his desk. She was a large, dark-faced lady, wrapped in a black coat and a plaid scarf, and clutching two small red mittens in her large hand. She explained that she had taken an unfurnished apartment and then bought some secondhand furniture and moved it in, and the landlord had then raised her rent because he said she was now living in a furnished apartment.

Canino threw his hands in the air.

"Abuses!" he shouted, "Abuses."

The woman looked down at the floor, trying to hold back a smile. The other ladies nudged one another.

Several more people had come in, and Canino's assistant had seated them and gone to the files to get out the records of those who had been there before. The pudgy young girl in the blue knee socks was still sitting idly at the long table, swinging her feet that did not quite touch the floor. Canino suddenly noticed her at a moment when he had taken off his glasses to stare around the room in the anguish of abuse, and asked, "Where is the typewriter?" The girl was still waiting for the typewriter to come so she could make out letters of complaint to the housing authority for many of the people present. She said she didn't know where the typewriter was. Canino jumped up and made a phone call, then sat down again, and said to the girl, "You see, we need two secretaries — full-time, regular secretaries, and a regular office on the ground floor. *That's* what we need."

The girl shyly nodded and looked away, her feet swinging faster above the floor.

About five minutes later the door opened and a boy about twelve years old walked in with a large portable typewriter.

"Eh, son," said Pedro Canino, rising from his desk with a great smile and going to embrace the boy. Canino's boy, a student at P.S. 108, was a quiet, handsome boy dressed in a gray coat and a natty gray cap. His large and serious brown eyes stared out from behind a pair of horn-rimmed glasses just like those his father wore. Canino lifted the typewriter onto the desk in front of the girl, and walked to the door with his son. He patted him proudly on the shoulders and returned to his desk, still smiling broadly.

The next citizen seeking help was a middle-aged lady with a drawn, sallow face and long, dark hair. She wore a black coat and white wool socks pulled high on her legs, and a red, white, and blue silk scarf tied tightly around her thin, pinched face. Her name was María Rodríguez. She told Canino that her husband had left her, and she and the four children were living on welfare. They lived in a single-room apartment at 84 East 108th Street and paid $18.26 rent every two weeks. There were cockroaches in the room and there was no steam heat. The children were sick, and their feet were swollen from the cold. She had complained to the landlord and the landlord said she was going to have to move. She appealed to the City Welfare Department for help in moving, and her welfare agent had left her a note written in English, which she couldn't read. She handed the note to Pedro Canino. It was scrawled in pen on stationery that was stamped with the words "City of New York Department of Welfare." It read as follows:

To: Mrs. Rodríguez. You will have to find your own apartment — you are now living in a furnished room, therefore
you don't need a truck to move you as you have no furniture.
When you find a new room inform the Department of Welfare at once.

It was signed with an indistinguishable signature, above a
line that said "Investigator."

Pete Canino stood up and pointed a finger at the other citizens, all of whom had leaned forward in their seats to hear the
story of Mrs. Rodríguez.

"You must come," said Canino quietly, "all of you, to a
meeting Thursday night at the school, P.S. 108, eight o'clock.
A man from the Rent Commission will be there."

Canino's voice rose and he said, "You must come and ask
embarrassing questions! I'll be there — all of you come!"

He sat down, pulled out a complaint form, and took down
the rest of the details from Mrs. Rodríguez. Mrs. Rodríguez
had no income of her own, and she was not eligible for an
apartment in a city housing project. Canino pressed out the
facts from his pen to the paper, and then told Mrs. Rodríguez
that later in the evening a *periodista* from one of the city's
English-language daily newspapers was coming around to see
the housing conditions, and he would take him to see Mrs.
Rodríguez's apartment and let the people read about it. Mrs.
Rodríguez said she'd be home.

The next lady in line was Mrs. Juana Escobar, who had
come in behalf of the people of her apartment building to file
a Multiple Tenants' Application for a Decrease in Rent.
These applications can be made stating complaints of violations in the apartment house and if the Rent Commission investigator finds them true, the rents will be ordered lowered

and the landlord will be forced into making the minimum repairs that the law necessitates.

Juana Escobar lived at 34-60 East 112th Street, a building
owned by one W. J. Kaufman, a landlord who has a great
many tenement buildings in East Harlem and has run them
with such professional disdain for the residents that his name
has become well known in Spanish Harlem. A person sometimes explains that he lives in "a Kaufman house," and the
listener will shake his head in sympathy. Kaufman was
brought to court on Christmas Eve of 1957 and got off with
$150 in fines. Perhaps the spirit of the season accounted for
the lenient punishment; it did not help the people who cele-
brated their holiday in the paint-flaking, rat-infested, un-
heated rooms that are so typical of his buildings.

The building that Juana Escobar lived in had twenty-eight
apartments. She began to state the complaints of herself and
her fellow tenants: defective plumbing, water faucets that
don't work, rats in the building, uncovered ratholes, broken
windows (the season was winter), warped walls, flaking paint,
not enough steam pressure to get hot water and heat to the top
floor, a broken skylight that let the rain in and soaked the
staircase, and several other minor items. Juana Escobar mentioned also that the superintendent waited until the coal supply
was completely exhausted before ordering more, and there
were therefore two or three days between the last of the supply and the delivery of the next when there was no heat at all.

By this time it was getting late, and Canino went from his
desk to talk to the people still waiting whom the lawyer or
assistants had not yet taken care of. As Canino was talking the
door opened and a crew-cut young man with a notebook entered and looked around the room. This was the *periodista*

from one of the city's daily newspapers, and Canino hurried over to grasp his arm in greeting. He pulled the reporter to a woman nearby and explained her case.

"People with problems!" Canino exclaimed, by way of introduction. "This poor woman, this woman lives in a one-room apartment and pays $80 a month and welfare only gives her $68 for rent so she has to take the rest from what she ought to use for food."

The woman nodded vigorously, and the reporter took her name and address. Shop was soon closed, and Canino set out with the reporter and another visitor to see some of the neighborhood apartments whose tenants had come to the Center that evening with complaints.

The night was cold, and a sharp wind swept down Madison Avenue — not the Madison Avenue of advertising and publishing firms in mid-Manhattan; not the Madison Avenue of fine apartments that form a clean canyon of stone to 96th Street. This was Madison Avenue "across the border" at 108th, where the streetlights grow sparse and the faces of the buildings are scarred and stained with the black and dingy marks of the tenements. There was hardly any traffic, and the streets were streaked with ribbons of the snow that had fallen the day before.

Canino led his visitors down 107th Street, and beckoned them up the stairs of an apartment house. The door of the building idly banged back and forth in the wind. Canino knocked at the first apartment inside, and he and his guests were welcomed by a woman who bade them come in, and began at once to explain her complaints in a torrent of Spanish. The newspaperman moved about with a pencil and notebook, glancing at the ceiling, into the corners, under the kitchen table. With his crew-cut, Ivy League appearance, his critical inspection suggested for the moment a college student looking over a room assigned him in some nightmare dormitory of the imagination. The floor was bare, and clothing was set in scattered piles around the room. The main piece of furniture was a mammoth television set that was placed near the window. The newspaperman stopped in his inspection to stare at it, then turned to the lady of the house and said, "You oughtn't to have that TV set — ought to buy the important things first." The woman, not understanding English, looked quizzically, respectfully, at the gentleman of the press, and he repeated his statement in a louder tone and somewhat more broken English. He turned then to Canino and said that he could spot no open housing violations. Canino said but there were rats in the place. The newspaperman said he hadn't detected any actual ratholes. Canino put this to the woman, who said that she didn't know about the holes but she knew her little boy had been bitten by rats. This news was translated by Canino, and the newspaperman brightened for a moment. He wondered if the woman would be willing to take her son to the Board of Health and show them the actual bite. The woman grimaced slightly when this was translated and said quietly that she thought she'd rather not do that. The reporter, dejected now, shook his head.

"Weak case," he said.

The visitors departed. They walked up the street to 108th, and turned in at No. 84, the building where María Rodríguez lived.

Pedro Canino knocked at Apartment 1, and María Rodríguez, her coat still wrapped around her, opened the door and stepped back to let the visitors enter. At the front of the room was a medium-sized bed with three little girls in it, covered by a ragged green blanket. On a couch next to them was another little girl. At the rear of the room a large blue flame waved up from a gas stove burner. This was the room's only heat. The radiators were stone-cold. There was no hot water.

María Rodríguez explained that the girls were too sick to go to school. Besides their feet being swollen, they all had colds. The reporter was inspecting a large hole in the floor under the washbasin. He asked Mrs. Rodríguez why she didn't complain to the superintendent. Mrs. Rodríguez said she did but it was hard and always unpleasant, for the superintendent had "a tongue like a sword." The visitors thanked Mrs. Rodríguez and turned to go. The eyes of the three little girls stared out from above the green blanket at the strangers. Their eyes were dark and curious and frightened; the eyes of their mother were dark and expressionless. She moved back silently beside the blue flame of the stove and folded her arms across her chest — a sibyl of the slums without heat or prophecy. Pedro Canino closed the door.

Down the hall in Apartment 2 the reporter found a very "strong case." There were holes in both the floor and the ceiling, big enough for the biggest rats. Cockroaches crawled up the kitchen wall. A curtain divided off a section of the room for a bedroom, and out from it peeked an old woman. She smiled at the visitors and watched them with interest. Isabel Sánchez, the head of the house, was pointing out more rat-holes. A teen-age girl sat staring at a television set whose screen was filled with a constantly wavering, almost undistinguishable cowboy movie, spoken in Spanish. The reporter walked to the kitchen to watch the cockroaches, and observed that some dishes were sitting on the table that contained the remains of rice and beans.

"Look here," the man from the newspaper said, "they haven't covered their food. They must cover their food. Pete, tell them they must do that."

Pete Canino talked about the holes in the ceiling, and looked for more. The reporter turned to the old woman who was staring from the curtain of the "bedroom."

"You must cover your food," he said in a loud voice.

The woman smiled.

Pete Canino thanked the occupants and led his visitors back to the street. The newspaperman wanted to see more apartments, and Pete explained that it was past eleven o'clock and almost everyone was asleep. There was a light on in a ground-floor apartment a few doors down, however, and Pete knocked on the window. A woman came to the door and explained in answer to Pete's questions the price and condition of her apartment. She said she complained and wasn't afraid to, because she had a regular job and supported herself, but the other tenants were afraid to complain because they were mostly on welfare and the superintendent threatened to kick them out if they complained and told them because they were on welfare he could kick them out whenever he wanted. It was not true, but the people were afraid to find out. The woman then asked if the two "Americans" with Pete were detectives. What else would two "Americans" be doing at night on East 108th Street?

Pete led the visitors away and said he was sorry he couldn't show them more, but most people were asleep now and he had to get to bed himself.

"I have to get up early tomorrow morning," he said. "I'm invited to a conference of the Christians and Jews. That's a wonderful organization, you know. Peoples, meeting together."

He bade goodbye and the strangers walked on, stopping for a moment to watch the train that suddenly thundered past on its way to Connecticut.

The following Thursday night Pete Canino closed his clinic to attend the PTA meeting at P.S. 108 where the man from the New York City Rent Commission was to talk and answer questions. There was a large turnout in the auditorium, more than a hundred men, women, and children. Pete Canino stalked up and down the aisles, quieting children, speaking to mothers, encouraging those whose troubles he knew to ask "embarrassing questions."

The speaker was Joseph Goldberg of the New York City Rent Commission. He had with him a Puerto Rican assistant from his office who was to act as translator. Mr. Goldberg began by explaining the concept of rent control. He told how rent control was started in 1943, and that whatever equipment and services the landlord provided then he was legally bound to provide now, for the same price rent.

"I know," Mr. Goldberg said, "that most of you people haven't lived in your apartment since 1943, however, and don't know what was provided then. One way to find out what you're entitled to is to find some neighbor who has been there since 1943 and have them tell you. If you can't find a neighbor who has been there that long, write to us and we'll tell you what you're entitled to. Write us at Lafayette Street."

The audience applauded, and the translator came to the microphone to put the instructions into Spanish. He too was applauded, and Mr. Goldberg took up the narrative again.

"Not all landlords are good landlords. Not all landlords are bad landlords. I will talk tonight just about the bad ones. Now a bad landlord is one who charges you more than the legal rent. If your rent, say, is $35 and he charges you more than that he is a bad landlord. If he charges you the correct rent, he may still be a bad landlord. That is, if he doesn't give you the services you are entitled to — for example, if a house has roaches and holes in the walls and the landlord doesn't do something about it, he is a bad landlord. Sometimes, a bad landlord wants to empty a house and change it so he can have an excuse to charge higher rents. There are apartments near here that rent for $25 a week for a room and a half after they have been 'modernized.' The landlord will try to evict you illegally by trying to scare you, by making life unpleasant, by not giving you heat and hot water. How can you defend yourself? Some landlords can frighten old people and those who don't know the language. Your defender is the Rent Commission. We will defend you. There isn't a landlord in New York that is not afraid of us. We can protect you . . ."

These remarks, and their translation, brought even greater applause. Mr. Goldberg continued: "It is not difficult to get help against a bad landlord. We have application forms you have to fill out. And there are organizations in this neighborhood that will help you fill out the applications. I believe that Mr. Canino has such an organization right close by here."

The audience turned and Mr. Canino waved and smiled from the back of the auditorium.

"We'll see that you get services or we'll lower the rent so much it doesn't pay the landlord not to make repairs. We'll also give you protection against a landlord who tries to put you out. Don't get panicked. If you're living peacefully in your apartment and paying your rent he can't put you out. If you have real trouble, come to our office. We're at 2 Lafayette Street. That's near City Hall."

After the translation, Mr. Goldberg was ready for the questions. A man at the front began to speak in Spanish with great excitement. The translator was called over, and he and Mr. Goldberg began talking with the man. There seemed to be some confusion. After four or five minutes, the rest of the audience began to grow restless. A few people left. Finally Mr. Goldberg went to the microphone.

"This tenant," he explained, "says that in 1956 the landlord put five radiators in his four-room apartment and got a rent increase. But the tenant says he doesn't need that many radiators. What should he have done? Unless the tenant writes a letter to me stating dissatisfaction with what happened, I can't do anything. My answer is — write to me directly!"

The tenant stood up again and began speaking excitedly in Spanish. Pete Canino got up and hurried down the aisle. He stopped about halfway and raised his hand.

"Excuse me please, Mr. Goldberg. I happen to know this case. It wasn't as you say. The problem was, the landlord put in five new radiators but only two of them worked. But he got the increase due for five. This man came to my clinic and we did write letters of complaint to the Rent Commission but nothing happened."

Mr. Goldberg stepped back and spoke for a moment with his Spanish translator. The tenant was up again, speaking rapidly in Spanish. Mr. Goldberg returned to the microphone and explained the difficulty of that case.

"It is impossible in a city the size of New York for things occasionally not to go wrong. I don't pretend to say that the Rent Commission is perfect. We try our best. I don't know this case but we will have the place reinspected. We'll take his name and address, and I'll have the inspector go there."

Mr. Goldberg paused for a moment and said, "When I asked you for questions, I didn't mean I could answer *particular* questions. I meant for you to ask *general* questions. Ones that will be of interest to everyone."

This perhaps was an example of the principle stated by Stanley H. Lowell, assistant to the mayor, when he told the Third Migration Conference in San Juan that the difficulties of Puerto Ricans would be lessened if they "gained more knowledge in advance of mainland customs and history." Were they familiar with mainland customs and history, they of course would have understood that "The City" and its representatives are not interested in particular problems, but general problems. The City is not interested in Isabel Sánchez and María Rodríguez. It is interested in "The Puerto Ricans."

The next question put to Mr. Goldberg — though it had its general application — was actually due to another misunderstanding of mainland customs.

"I want to know," a lady asked, "why the landlord doesn't keep his promises."

There were only two other questions, both helpfully general, and then Mr. Goldberg said, "I think I'll end this little talk. I want to compliment you all for the attention given me. I'm most grateful to the little children."

The audience rose and dispersed, returning again to the particular apartments where they and their families live with particular rats and particular cockroaches and particular children whose particular feet are swollen from the lack of heat in a particular cold radiator.

When, oh when, will they learn the customs of the mainland?

The customs they must forge for themselves in moving into

Spanish Harlem are the customs of survival in housing whose decayed and crowded conditions are extreme enough to be almost unique — not only on the U.S. mainland but also in the world. Charles Abrams, the head of the New York State Commission Against Discrimination and a foremost housing authority, circled the globe in 1954 on a UN housing mission, and his points of comparison in housing conditions in East Harlem were with "the submarginal areas of Asia and Africa." Mr. Abrams reported his findings in *Commentary* Magazine in 1955, saying:

> In the last twelve months I have traveled some 75,000 miles on housing missions for the UN. With some embarrassment I have had to conclude that the slums in Harlem where most Puerto Ricans have found shelter are among the worst in the world. In the submarginal areas of Asia and Africa, economic conditions are, of course, often less critical. There is the redeeming feature of a warm climate; the crowding per acre is usually less; there is often an external environment which offsets the squalor of the house itself . . .

Since most Puerto Ricans in New York City live in slum conditions, it is part of the popular myth of their migration that they created the slums. The truth is, rather, they inherited the slums. East Harlem was a hovel unsuitable for human life long before the great postwar migration from the island filled it to overflowing and made it one of the most crowded living areas in the world. As long ago as 1939 a New York citizens' housing council observed in East Harlem "widescale dilapidation and progressive blight reflected in the increasing number of vacant and boarded properties and demolished buildings. With the exception of a few blocks scattered here and there throughout the area, and on Fifth Avenue facing Central Park, all sections of East Harlem reveal advanced property dilapidation."

Those dilapidated buildings were the ghosts of the country's first great waves of immigration. The sudden growth of New York City, expanded by arrivals of immigrants from Europe in the nineteenth century, called for a rapid development of housing, the quickest and the cheapest kind. Harlem was one of the main spots where the rush of low-rent multiple dwellings began to cover the once suburban landscape. These apartment houses, built before 1901, are now officially known as "old-law tenements," and in the mid-1950's there were still more than 50,000 such buildings in the city, housing more than 400,000 families, mostly Negro and Puerto Rican.

Even when the old-law tenements were brand-new — that is, before the turn of the century — they were far from being anyone's dream of Home. The rationale of the design was to provide the greatest use of the lot. Neither the comfort nor even the sanitation of the tenants was taken into consideration. At the time these structures were built the indoor toilet was still something of a luxury, and in the buildings where toilet facilities were installed they were rarely in each apartment, but more often one to a floor — a "hall toilet" for the use of all the families on the floor. Inside rooms, normally cited for use as bedrooms, had no windows and depended on the adjoining room for fresh air. On the outside, no thought was given to making the face of the building attractive, or even uniquely ugly in a way that at least was different from the rest. The standard city tenements are too familiar to need any further description; you have seen their faces.

The single advantage these mass-produced cells had to offer

was the one advantage most important to the city's new arrivals — low rent. The final irony of a half century later is that many of them no longer offered even that to the Puerto Ricans, who had little choice but to take them as a home. Many have been converted to "rooming houses" that charge as much as $100 a month for a single room.

There was an era during the latter half of the twenties and through the thirties when the old-law tenements seemed to be fated to pass from the scene— even in Harlem. A Mayor's Committee on City Planning in 1937 observed in an East Harlem Community Study that the old-law tenements standing in the area were no longer the easy profit makers they had been. Many of the most decayed were boarded up. Although there was a Puerto Rican community in the neighborhood at that time, as well as Italian and Jewish sections, many of the former residents from older immigration waves, including Irish, Italian, and Jewish, had been able to make the move up the ladder to better quarters, and the area was not as crowded as it once had been. And, in the most crowded tenement conditions that the early immigrants suffered through, they at least had the relative advantages of low rents and the fact that the tenement buildings were still not a half century old. It was thus possible for Charles Abrams to state with discouraging accuracy in the mid-fifties that "even in the period between 1900 and the 1920s, when housing conditions for immigrants were bad, they were hardly comparable to those encountered by the Puerto Rican newcomers today."

The slack period in immigration and the movement of the older immigrants out of East Harlem that brought about the temporary ease in tenement conditions was abruptly ended after World War II. Then the great waves of workers followed the call of employment, up from Puerto Rico and the southern United States, and both Negroes and Puerto Ricans began to pour into New York City — and, especially, into East Harlem.

By the mid-1950's, the roughly mile-square area of East Harlem was one of the world's most densely populated areas. It was estimated that nearly 300,000 people lived in that space. On a single, dark block — East 100th Street between First and Second Avenues — there were more than 4000 human beings jammed into 27 ancient tenements. It is hardly surprising that this block has come to be known by police as "the worst block in the city" from the standpoint of crime and narcotics addiction. People who have lived on the block and been unable to move out of East Harlem are often relieved to be able at least to move away from 100th Street. One young man who moved from 100th to 106th Street counts his success in staying out of trouble and holding a job to the six-block move he made. Pee-Wee Leon, one of the prime movers of the Neighborhood Narcotics Committee, was recently able to move from 100th Street to a project farther up in East Harlem, and lives with the relief that his children don't have to grow up on the same deadly block that he did.

In the sudden postwar swell of population that filled an already crowded 100th Street into still more crowded conditions, and as the same thing happened all over East Harlem, the unused old-law tenements again were unboarded, and opened their dilapidated doors to a new group of strangers. City officials this time saw little hope of their being torn from the landscape within the foreseeable future. The Mayor's Committee for Better Housing Report (Subcommittee on Old Law Tenements) summed up the situation this way in 1955 (italics our own, emphasizing the more "philo-sophical" aspects of the report):

> As long as low income persons and families continue to pour into the city from the south and from Puerto Rico *and are content to live under conditions that to our modern civic conscience educated to higher housing standards appear intolerable*, there will be such demand for cheap housing that the old law tenement will remain as a very undesirable part of our city housing supply.

It is doubtful of course that any of the authors who wrote this report are acquainted with anyone who lives in the old-law tenements they talk about. It is doubtful that any of them ever passed an evening at Pete Canino's Civic Orientation Center and talked with the people who came for help. It would be very interesting for them to spend such an evening, and take a poll of how many citizens present were content with their housing. The picture of María Rodríguez standing beside the blue gas flame that provided her only heat and the three children who stared from beneath the moth-eaten blankets of the room's only bed was not a picture of content-ment. María Rodríguez needs no such abstraction as a modern civic conscience to find her apartment intolerable; she needs nothing more than the sight of her children.

The citizens who might more reasonably search for a modern civic conscience are the landlords who make their living from renting these rotted holes. The profits are tremendous.

Purchase of the tenement buildings is cheap and usually yields 30 to 100 per cent a year on the original investment. The upkeep is cheap, because there usually is none. If the tenant complains, the landlord threatens to move him out, and depends on the tenant's ignorance and fear as a stranger to the city and its laws to be able to hold such a threat, which is actually illegal. But the landlord also has a legal threat — if too many complaints cause too close inspection on a badly deteriorated building, it may be condemned. When faced with a choice of bad conditions or condemnation of the building, the tenant must keep silent, for if the building is ordered vacant it means he is out on the street again. No matter how bad the building, it is better than the street.

Although landlords are sometimes brought to court on housing violations, the maximum fine for landlord violations of building regulations is $500, and the fines are seldom more than a few hundred dollars, even in the most extreme cases. The profit of the building easily pays that as part of the "overhead." In many cases the profits of a tenement apartment are multiplied, along with the woes of its tenants, when the landlord subdivides it into more rooms. This is often done also in buildings that are in reasonably good condition and would make fairly comfortable places to live. By putting in flimsy wooden panels and creating twice as many segments or "rooms" a landlord can have that much more rent. Such rooms are often rented to Puerto Ricans and Negroes who can find nothing else. The building of course becomes quickly dilapidated with the overcrowding, and soon it is said by passers-by that "the Puerto Ricans have ruined the building."

It often happens that a landlord rents one of these rooms to a family of three or four or more persons. Then, if the people complain of bad plumbing, rats, or other violations, the landlord can tell them to go ahead and report it, but if they do, he can have them removed for illegal occupancy by reporting that he rented the room to one person and others moved in without his permission.

As the nightmare conditions of the tenements increase, so does the cost of living in them. It is difficult, if not impossible, to find an apartment in East Harlem without paying a "bonus" that usually goes to the landlord. One young married couple several years ago had to pay $1400 for the kitchen tables and chairs in a tenement apartment in order to rent it. In 1954 the East Harlem Protestant Parish started a better-housing campaign, and began with a survey in which 1000 people in the neighborhood answered questions about their apartments. One of the questions was whether or not the tenant had to pay a bonus to get the apartment, and how much the bonus was. One hundred and nineteen people admitted to paying bonuses that totaled $60,952.00.

The better-business maxim, "You get what you pay for," may hold true for the work of the spirits in Spanish Harlem, but it doesn't apply to housing. The type of housing the people got who paid the exorbitant bonus fees was indicated in the rest of the answers on the Parish questionnaire. Out of the 1000 tenants interviewed, the following numbers of housing violations were reported: defective wiring, 721; defective plumbing, 612; windows broken, 571; rats in the building, 895; gas leaks, 696; no heat, 778; no hot water, 553; leaks in roof, 308 . . .

The battle of the Parish to better these conditions, with its full staff, outside friends, and people of the neighborhood joining together in the fight, was a slow and uphill story that gives some indication of the chances a single individual has of getting the minimum living requirements in a tenement apartment.

The tenants of 331 East 100th Street joined together with the help of Parish ministers and lawyers to get the minimum standards of heat, hot water, and long overdue repairs. The heat and hot water were gotten fairly quickly. It took three years and the advent of a new landlord before the basic repairs were made.

In an even more Kafka-like case, the Parish pitched in to help the tenants of a rooming house on East 106th Street. There were 16 rooms, 16 families, 20 children, and 3 bathrooms in the building. Rents were from $12 to $20 a week. Tenants had asked for rent receipts and none had received any for two years. At the time the Parish came in to help, there had been no heat or hot water for two weeks and no gas or electricity for one week. The landlord had a $384.55 utility bill that he refused to pay.

The Parish began to make the rounds of city agencies to get some action. A lawyer and minister called on the New York State Rent Commission, the District Attorney's office, the Department of Housing and Buildings, the Health Department, the Chief Magistrate's office, the Department of Welfare, the Mayor's office, and Consolidated Edison. After making those rounds the first time, there was still no relief for the tenants. The Rent Commission sent inspectors and threatened to reduce the rents to $1 a month beginning the following week. The District Attorney's office could do nothing without a complaint from Consolidated Edison that the landlord had been stealing gas and electricity from them. Consolidated Edison refused to take any action through the District Attorney's office because it felt the publicity would be unfavorable. It also refused to accept payments from a tenants' pool backed by the credit of the East Harlem Protestant Parish to turn the service back on. The Department of Housing and Buildings issued a summons against the landlord returnable the following week. The Department of Health sent an inspector and promised to testify in court. But the tenants still had no heat, hot water, gas, or electricity. They had to wait until the following week when the case came to court. At last, with the help of eight different city and state agencies, the services were turned back on for these tenants, many of whom were paying $80 a month rent.

There is no place so costly to live as a tenement. To do it with any security, a man would need a staff of lawyers, priests, seers, repairmen, accountants, and secretaries. He might then be able to insure his rights and a minimum standard of living.

How does a single individual — especially an individual who is strange to the city, who perhaps cannot speak its language — insure for himself the minimum requirements of life he is paying for when it takes a staff of ministers and lawyers weeks and weeks and visits to eight different city, state, and private agencies to get the gas and light turned on in a single apartment? The people in all those agencies are working hard, but they are working hard, by necessity, for a faceless plural. They are like Joseph Goldberg, a dedicated man, who could only tell his audience at P.S. 108 that he was there to answer "general" questions. To see a single face is to allow the system and procedure to collapse.

The ministers and members of the East Harlem Protestant Parish, living as they do in the neighborhood, deal only with individuals. That is what made their campaign for better housing so complicated when it had to deal with official government agencies. It was not the easy matter of good fighting evil, but the much more complex and frustrating matter of fighting for individual good against abstract good.

When blocks and blocks of tenements were razed to put up

a new City Housing Project, no one could deny that it was all to the good. The housing projects perhaps represent the greatest "abstract good" in the neighborhood, and almost by definition then, one of the people's most complex and frustrating problems. When the city condemned the old tenement buildings, it sent the former residents who were eligible to other projects throughout the city and got temporary rooms in nearby tenements that later would be razed for the people who couldn't qualify for other places. The family that does not meet city qualifications for a project and that lives in a tenement condemned to be razed is thus sent to the next condemned tenement owned by the city that may not be razed for another year or so. When that one is razed, the family is sent to another city-owned tenement, and so on. A new category of citizens is created — those people who move from condemned site to condemned site, in a seemingly endless round. These government-propelled travelers are referred to as "Site Migrants."

A group of these citizens who were moved from a new project site in East Harlem and could not qualify for living in any city projects were stuck in a city-owned tenement in an advanced state of decay near one of the Parish churches. The Parish sponsored a protest meeting with the City Housing Authority to ask that these people be placed in some project or found minimum-standard living quarters. The meeting brought face to face the Authority and the individuals. The Reverend Norman Eddy described it this way:

"We had the protest meeting about the 5 per cent or so people left over who could get in none of the projects and who were living in these miserable buildings in the worst of conditions. The Housing Authority had five or six men at the meeting, and they were honest, sincere, dedicated men — they certainly weren't villains, and it was hard to get mad at them. It's easy to get mad at a landlord who's just out to make his buck, and it's easy to fight him, but these men were obviously good people. And yet they couldn't see the thing in human terms. They thought it was wonderful that only 5 per cent were left in this mess. They didn't seem to see that there were individuals who made up that 5 per cent. There was an old woman living in the building who was all alone except for a dog she kept — that was her family. She wouldn't give up the dog and so she couldn't be accepted into a project. No animals are allowed. The Housing people couldn't understand this. They just said, 'Well, tell her to get rid of the dog.' But the dog was all she had."

The impersonal good and personal evil of the housing projects continue after the structures are built; matching in essence the blank, ugly, strong, clean, identical faces of the buildings themselves. How ironically close are the aims and results of the projects and the tenements! Both were built to accommodate the greatest numbers possible; both were built with mass-production, standard design, with no reference to the world they stand in. And yet the tenements were built for the benefit of landlords; the projects for the benefit of "the people."

Angry outside critics have cried that "the people" have proved themselves unworthy of these cheap, sallow-stone monsters of shelter. Projects have quickly deteriorated; there has been no "pride" in upkeep or appearance. How ungrateful are the careless tenants — how unworthy of these subsidized homes!

But the rules that govern the housing projects eliminate any possible conception of them as a home. The idea of a home implies permanence and roots. The rules that govern the project make it not a home but a cheap hotel; its tenants the always potential nomads whose wanderings can be set in motion by a mimeographed notice from the Housing Authority. Admittance to a project and survival in it are determined by the number of persons in the family and the total family income. To start with, a single person who happened to live on a site razed for a project would not be able to live in the new building because the federal public housing law does not consider a single person as a family unit. It further does not consider anyone outside the immediate family as a part of the family unit. Thus a family that has cousins, nephews, nieces, an old boarder who has come to be thought of as "part of the Family" or even grandchildren living with a grandparent, is ineligible for the housing project. If a family suits the qualifications and is moved into a project, changes in the family may move them out again. If a husband and wife move in and the husband leaves, the wife must face not only the problems of a new life alone, perhaps a divorce, but also eviction. She is no longer a "family unit" and thus not eligible for a project.

Perhaps the most terrifying type of case has occurred when tenants were evicted on the grounds that some member of the family was "undesirable." Anyone who has committed a crime is "undesirable." Thus if a son is arrested for possession of narcotics, the whole family may be evicted from the apartment. In one case in East Harlem, a boy was picked up on a murder charge involving a teen-age gang, and in this time of trouble for the family they received a notice of eviction from the City Housing Authority. The son was in jail — not in the apartment — and he had not yet been tried or convicted, but the family was ordered to leave the project. In the spring of 1958 the New York *Post* discovered that in the past year 170 families had been evicted from city housing projects without being told the charges against them but merely that they were "undesirable." The families were unable to protest the evictions in Municipal Term Court. The magistrates ruled that the court could not look into the charges because a Tenants Review Board of the City Housing Authority had already done so and issued the evictions. None of the families were able to appear before the Review Board. Test cases were taken before the New York State Supreme Court, which ruled against the action of the Housing Authority, and the procedure was stopped until a final legal clarification of the matter was made.

But the much more common cause of fear and tension over eviction is income. Every project has its fixed income rates that the family cannot exceed. A typical one was released in the announcement for the Washington Houses in East Harlem. A form letter announcing opening for applications stated that income eligibility would be passed if the total family income was:

> Under $2800 for a 2-person family.
> Under $3100 for a 3-person family.
> Under $3200 for a 4-person family.
> Under $3600 for a 5-person family.
> Under $3700 for a 6-person family.

These are not only entrance requirements — they are ceilings whose passage is grounds for eviction. If a man with a family in a private home or apartment gets a raise, it means he has the chance to improve his home. If a man in a project gets a raise, it means he may have to move out of his home.

There must be uncountable cases like the man with a wife and three children who lives in the East River Houses, makes $3000 a year, and has been notified that the next raise he gets will put him over the ceiling for the project and mean automatic eviction. It so happens he works for the City; his next raise will be automatic, after a certain length of time on the job. When, as his boss, the city government automatically raises his salary, it will, as his landlord, automatically kick him out of his apartment.

The father of another project family earns $45 a week. He is not a city employee and he sees no chance of getting a raise. His son, however, has recently graduated from high school and wants to get a job. His salary, added to the total family income, will mean eviction for the family. In many families, the parents are anxious for the children to hold some minor job, which, in this turbulent neighborhood, may keep them off the streets and out of trouble. But the small added income often means eviction, and the parents must reluctantly forbid the children to take a part-time job.

These are among the rules of life in the slums of Spanish Harlem. They are part of the required, no-credit course in orientation to the strange and deadly customs of the mainland.

The Bible study class was discussing the Book of Job, and talking about how the problems in it related to the problems of the people in Spanish Harlem. Someone ventured the opinion that perhaps God wanted them to live in this neighborhood to test their faith. One young man slammed his Bible shut, leaned forward, and spoke with intense conviction: "I say it's not God or the Devil that put us here, I say it's Society."

The Invisible Man

Y los últimos serán los primeros . . . (And the last
shall be the first)

> — From a campaign leaflet of
> José Lumen Román, candidate
> for the New York City Council

A HALF-DOZEN MEN wearing wide, straw-thatched sombreros
walked through the rain of an autumn Thursday night on
East 104th Street and turned inside the Union Settlement
House. They entered the auditorium, paused for a moment,
and looked from left to right. On the left-hand side ten
people, all but two of them white, were scattered through
the rows of folding chairs. Most of them sat alone. On the
right-hand side about fifty people, several of them wearing
the wide sombreros, were sitting together — some chattering
among themselves in Spanish, others waiting with folded hands
and a silent, skeptical detachment. The half-dozen men who
had just come in walked quickly to the right and looked for
seats. They did not take off the sombreros they wore, and
the inscriptions painted in red across the crown of each one
— "*Vota José Lumen Román*" — were fixed, as were the
faces beneath them, on the men who moved against the brown
velvet backdrop curtain on the stage. These were the sponsors
and principal speakers of the evening's program, which

brought for the first time in anyone's memory the candidates for city council in the heart of East Harlem together at the same time and place to discuss the issues of the coming campaign.

This in itself was enough to make the meeting a notable event for the neighborhood; its consequences were further enlarged by the fact that one of the candidates present — the man whose name appeared on the crowns of the sombreros — was aspiring to be the first Puerto Rican in history to win a seat on the New York City Council. When José Lumen Román opened his hopefully historic campaign in the fall of 1957, Puerto Ricans had lived in New York for more than a century, and the more than half-million residents of Puerto Rican birth or parentage made New York the largest city of Puerto Ricans in the world, including San Juan. And yet, no Puerto Rican had ever gained one of the twenty-five seats on the New York City Council, or, for that matter, any elective city office.

The man who had tossed his sombrero in the ring for the City Council seat from East Harlem was a thirty-two-year-old reporter for *El Diario de Nueva York* who lived in the Bronx. For purposes of his political ambition Román took an address on East 100th Street, between First and Second Avenues, but was seldom seen on the block. When asked once why he didn't move to the neighborhood he hoped to represent, Román raised his hands palms up in desperation and explained, "I have three children." No political office is high enough to make a father voluntarily move his family to 100th Street. This did not work toward a grass-roots wave of sentiment for José Román among the 4000 people who lived on the block, but only a few of that number were ever aware of his supposed presence, or, indeed, his campaign. Some of those who knew what was going on had too much experience in local political matters to think twice about the issue of residency — rare indeed is the political representative of this neighborhood who actually lives in it.

A much greater potential handicap for Román than the fact that he didn't live in the district was the fact that he had been, in addition to his duties for *El Diario,* the master of ceremonies of a Spanish-language TV version of "Mr. Anthony" called "What Is Your Problem?" Many Puerto Ricans objected to the program because they felt it exploited and advertised the problems of the Puerto Ricans and further lowered their status and reputation as a group. Problems common to all humanity were paraded before the microphone, and many Puerto Rican watchers felt that the presentation implied that these were all "Puerto Rican problems." They especially objected to the fact that the problems would be laid bare in all their terror, and then an advertisement for roach spray would be flashed on the screen. All this has its bitter effects when presented to a group made sensitive to their public image by the daily experience of being a "Spic" in a city of strangers. But Román was at least widely known, no matter what the final judgment of his public, through his articles in *El Diario.* Román was the first reporter to write on the exploitation of Puerto Ricans in racket unions in New York City, and he later testified on the matter before the McClellan Committee.

As for previous political experience, Joe Román was an innocent. He had come to the States only eight years before from Puerto Rico to go to the school of journalism at Long Island University, and his grasp of the inner workings of national or even city politics was hardly that of an old-time resident, much less an old-time politician. But all these questions were secondary to the main facts that Román was known, and, most important of all, Román was a Puerto Rican. Many of his posters and leaflets carried with their messages the simple, significant inscription, "*De Boricua . . . A Boricua*" (From a Puerto Rican . . . To a Puerto Rican). This was the issue.

It was mainly Puerto Ricans who followed Román's meetings and speeches, and it was mainly Puerto Ricans who attended the historic meeting at the Union Settlement House to hear the local candidates for city council. Many of the people who came could speak only Spanish, but all the audience sat attentively as speakers in English told them the importance of political action. The word came first from God, as represented by a local minister called in to act as an "impartial" master of ceremonies (the implication being the essentially sacrilegious one that God would be impartial in matters such as these) and next from Organized Labor, as represented by the New York Hotel Trades Council, an organization whose union members of hotel and restaurant workers are composed of a growing number of Puerto Ricans, and whose local committee sponsored the evening's unusual meeting.

As if the evening's historic and inspirational atmosphere was not impressive enough already, it turned out that not only God and Organized Labor were represented on the stage, but the Republican Party as well. God nearly always has an agent at East Harlem gatherings, and the unions are showing up more and more often, but Republicans seldom venture into that part of the 22nd Senatorial District north of 96th Street. When anyone in the neighborhood mentions The Conservatives, they are referring not to politicians but to the teen-age gang that went social. But sitting on the Union Settlement stage, big as life and swathed in the blackest flannel, was Richard C. Welden, the young lawyer chosen as the year's Republican sacrifice in the 22nd District.

Everyone seemed to understand the ethereal nature of Welden's appearance, including Welden, who took the floor first because he had to get on to another appointment. The audience almost automatically began to grow restless as he presented his brief, which dealt with the topic he judged this gathering to be most interested in — the bill to eliminate discrimination in New York City housing. Welden was against discrimination: "I think all candidates for political office in New York City are against discrimination." The joy of being residents of such an enlightened capital seemed to be lost on the crowd, but Welden forged on undaunted, droning out readings of various anti-discrimination laws as an agent on the right-hand side of the room got up to pass out additional sombreros painted with "Vota José Lumen Román."

The audience no doubt knew without paying the close attention that the text required that Welden after all had his reservations about integration. He recommended holding off the anti-bias housing bill in favor of "voluntary integration" which really was the best and most amiable course. "That is my position," he said in conclusion. "I hope you understand it is not ambiguous."

It really was not, and there was no applause. Several perfunctory questions came from the audience, amidst much shuffling, when suddenly there arose from the right-hand side of the room a man with black hair, a black mustache, a large black umbrella, and rimless glasses that matched his severe expression. Although unknown to Welden, this was William

Rodríguez Carrasquillo, campaign manager of José Lumen Román, and he demanded to know if anyone on the left-hand side of the room spoke Spanish. The two Negroes and eight white people scattered through that section looked up expressionless, without a single "*Sí*," and Rodríguez asked the chair if this very meeting was not the moment to begin integration. There was hearty applause as Willie Rodríguez hoisted his great umbrella and moved to the other side. A heavy Italian man in a gray sweater and rumpled brown overcoat in turn heaved up from his lonely seat on the left and walked over to join the Puerto Ricans on the right, accompanied by another burst of applause. In the midst of this democratic action Richard Welden, sensing that he had lost the initiative, picked up his briefcase, nodded farewell to the unmindful audience, and disappeared into the night.

The voluntary integration and disappearance of Welden seemed to have a happy effect on the audience, and when José Lumen Román, candidate of the Liberal Party, came to the front of the stage, the atmosphere had lost much of its tension. The coming of Román further increased the friendly spirit. He stood at one side of the stage, an almost tiny man with a pale, serious face, supporting large, black-rimmed glasses. He wore as usual a bow tie and a dark single-breasted suit, and resembled in dress and manner a patient young professor about to lead his class through the difficulties of the latest assignment. As he speaks, his head tilts slightly to one side, his face in a heavily serious concentration that pleads for attention. He began, speaking in English, saying that he had offered to act as an interpreter at this meeting for Welden and John J. Merli, the Democratic candidate, since he knew that many of the people present spoke only Spanish and the other two candidates did not.

"But who," said Román, "will be present day in and day out on the City Council to interpret the needs of the Puerto Rican citizens if these men are elected?"

The audience cheered, and Román told them that "the issue in this campaign is Puerto Rican representation. There are over 500,000 Puerto Ricans in New York and not one is on the City Council."

Román warmed up to his subject, bringing his arms down in quick public-speaking gesture jerks of emphasis, recounting the sad conditions in which the Puerto Ricans were forced to live, in tenements where "roaches are as large as mice and rats are as big as cats." The audience who lived in the tenements laughed and clapped at the exaggeration of size, if not of fact. Things are never so bad but what they couldn't be bigger.

As for his opponent, the incumbent councilman John J. Merli, Román charged that this representative of the people was always absent when it came to important votes: "His oldest trick is to disappear." John Merli sat expressionless on the stage as the audience laughed at the allusion to the name their councilman is known by among the Puerto Ricans of his district: "Merli, the Invisible Man."

"I call," said Román, "for a sign in the City Council that says for the first time in New York City's history: '*Aquí se habla español*.'"

The campaign sombreros were waved in the air and Román smiled at the cheers. A tall, aged man with deep lines running through his dark brown face got up from the back of the room and asked in Spanish if the questions had to be asked in English. The crowd on the right cried "*Español!*" A translator was brought out, and by the curious protocol that had been decided on, stood by to translate the questions asked him in

Román's native tongue into English for José Lumen Román.

A pretty young woman in a blue silk dress arose and addressed the stage in Spanish. The translator told Román that the lady's question was why the Americans hated the Puerto Ricans. She did not understand why it should be, or why it was that landlords and Italians had such a special hate for Puerto Ricans.

José Román was graceful enough not to refer the question to John Merli, the political leader of East Harlem's Italians and champion of its landlords.

"Only low, uneducated people hate the Puerto Ricans," Román answered. "True Americans don't dislike Puerto Ricans."

This news was translated into Spanish, whereupon a man got up and asked then if newspapermen were not true Americans.

Román did the best he could with these ideological questions, and wound up with more clear-cut assurances on practical matters, such as promise of protection to building superintendents, who often were tossed out with only a few days' notice by the landlords without explanation or compensation. The economic "issues" had begun to take shape: as a candidate of the Puerto Ricans, the city's newest minority group, Román was pledged to protect the superintendents. As a candidate of the Italians, who have now been residents long enough to realize fully the American dream, Merli was pledged to protect the landlords.

Román, having fully assured his followers of safeguarding their particular interests, turned the floor over to the landlords' freedom fighter. Councilman Merli was of course psychologically handicapped by the fact that he was standing in the camp of the enemy. Italians have long ago stopped attending political affairs at this "mass" level in East Harlem, for they long ago captured it and have long owned it, politically and economically. The best guess on Merli's appearance at this event was professional curiosity as to what the new, never yet seriously insurgent Puerto Ricans were up to. They cannot yet be taken too seriously in this, their oldest neighborhood in the city, for they are far from owning it; they only live in it.

John J. Merli, "The Invisible Man" made flesh, stepped to the front of the stage — a large, blue-suited man with glasses and thinning gray hair and a voice as husky as his body that seemed uncomfortably strapped in its meeting-night clothes. He told the audience with injured pride that he was after all no outsider: "I have spoken in this hall many times. Over fifty-three years ago I was born three blocks away from here. I still live in the room where I was born."

Besides these qualifications of residency, Merli reminded the crowd: "I come from a minority group *too*. My father came from Italy — steerage."

This was the comparative credential of an ancestor on the *Mayflower* for a candidate running at a D.A.R. convention — even more, it was the pride of the father who woke to a pitcher of ice for bathing and walked four miles to school in the winter and scoffs at his son's complaints about homework. Merli's father came steerage on the high Atlantic; the Puerto Ricans come by plane from the San Juan airport — and yet they complain.

Merli went on to shout out the numbers of the bills he had sponsored in the City Council; and taking note of the nature of most of them, paused to point a finger at the audience **and** say, "I'm proud of the fight I've waged for the small business-man. You in this room are mostly laborers now, but in five, ten, fifteen years, God willing — you'll be able to buy a small business yourself."

John Merli, almost breathless now, rested his case with the promise of Democratic capitalism, and opened the floor for questions.

Willie Rodríguez, bearing his black umbrella like a lance, popped up and asked if Mr. Merli realized the tremendous in-flux of Puerto Ricans into East Harlem, and into all New York. Merli admitted to this knowledge and Willie pressed on to ask whether or not these people shouldn't have a repre-sentative on the City Council. Merli judged that this was a loaded question, and felt that he had to answer yes, if they felt a Puerto Rican would represent them better than himself, they of course should elect one. The councilman drew his first and only cheer of the evening.

A young man in a leather jacket got up and asked Mr. Merli if he believed in working six days and then going to church and resting on the seventh. Mr. Merli said he found no fault with that program, and followed it himself. "Well then," the young man wanted to know, "you think it's right I have to work sixty-seventy hours a week myself?"

Mr. Merli looked startled and informed the young man that the sixty-hour week had long been legislated off the books.

"But what am I going to do about it?" the young man asked.

Mr. Merli said he should by all means take it to the proper authorities. The audience laughed; they had been there be-fore. The people's representative had held up to them the hope of buying a small business, but the people were hoping for a six-day week.

A lady got up to say that the Puerto Ricans needed help,

and Mr. Merli said his political club was open every Monday and Thursday night from eight o'clock on. The lady asked if Mr. Merli spoke Spanish, and he admitted his vocabulary was limited to several phrases he remembered from high school. The question of whether the lady or her friends could get much help from Merli's club will remain hypothetical because the lady and her friends will not go. They will not trust their problems to Italians and landlords.

The questions ended, and the audience filed back out to 104th Street — the more dedicated partisans of José Lumen Román having at least the advantage of the campaign sombreros that served an unexpected practical purpose in keeping the rain off the heads of the wearers. The wide sombreros that served as a symbol of Román's battle are first of all the symbol of the Puerto Rican worker of the hills, the *jíbaro*: symbol of the poverty the people of the island thought they were leaving behind and were ashamed of and found in a different form in New York City. They appealed, as did Román's entire campaign and platform, to the sense of "national" unity and indignation, and in that sense became a symbol also of the campaign's bitter, predestined finale.

The campaign of José Román to win a seat on the New York City Council was launched with a speech by the mayoress of San Juan, and closed with a speech by one of Román's workers calling for the formation of a "Spanish Party" in local politics. In all the bright oratory of opening night at Román's headquarters on 106th and Lexington, a representative of the Liberal Party apologized for not being able to address the audience in Spanish as the Puerto Rican speakers were doing, but observed that "after all, we are all Americans."

The observation was legally accurate, but as the campaign

progressed it became increasingly obvious that the legal truth was in reality a political lie. On the week end before the election, campaign manager Willie Rodríguez dolefully stared at the map on the wall of the 22nd Senatorial District in New York City and reviewed the battle. There is one member on the City Council from each of the twenty-five senatorial districts in the city; the 22nd, where Román waged his campaign, runs roughly from East 74th Street as far north as East 135th Street, from the East River to Park Avenue, with a bulge in the middle that extends as far west as Eighth Avenue. The world of Spanish Harlem occupies the heart of the area, with Puerto Ricans living throughout all the district north of 96th Street. But south of 96th is the old German community of Yorkville, in the east, and the upper reaches of the heavily Republican "Silk Stocking" district in the west, around Madison and Park Avenues. In the northeast corner of the district, around 116th and First Avenue running north, is the last of the old Italian stronghold.

Willie Rodríguez, examining the map of this great "melting pot" of the nation, explained that his people had conducted their campaign mainly in the "Spanish" part of it.

"What we wanted to do," he said, "was get speakers to go into the other sections — German speakers in the German section, Italian in the Italian, and over here, this is a rich district, have an American speaker go. The trouble is, we lack the speakers. We go in ourselves, they can tell the accent right away — it's no good. We did get one Italian girl to help us though — very nice girl. She was out last night giving speeches in Italian."

In the meantime, candidate Román, having covered the "Spanish" section of the district, was speaking to a Puerto

Rican Merchants Association on 14th Street, and preparing to give a pre-election week-end address to a Puerto Rican group in the Bronx. They of course could not cast a single vote for him, but contributed their full moral support.

This concept of sectional campaigning was not originated by José Lumen Román — it is an old East Harlem inheritance. The only politician who brought the minority groups of the area together for any political cause was Vito Marcantonio — though his technique was hardly a violation of the tradition. Marcantonio merely learned all the languages of all the large minority groups in his district — Italian, English, Yiddish, and Spanish.

Marcantonio, who caused another unusual political union when the Republican, Democrat, and Liberal Parties joined in a coalition to oust him finally from his seat as East Harlem's U.S. Representative in 1950 after he had established a firm reputation as follower of the Communist Party line in Congress, was and still is a legend in his old neighborhood. The five thousand people who attended his funeral in 1954 were made up of people who spoke all the languages he did, and several others. Once during the campaign of José Román a group on a street corner in the heart of East Harlem's Puerto Rican district stopped several people and asked them who was the politician who had done the most for the Puerto Ricans. The answers were either Marcantonio or no one. One man reached in his billfold and pulled out a lifetime membership card in the Vito Marcantonio Club. Nearly every old-time resident has a story — often improved by the passage of time — of how the great "Marc" saved him from a landlord, or personally came to his apartment to turn on the steam, or examined a damaged stair and demanded its repair. His popu-

larity prompted dire prophecies and speculations in the outside world — outside of East Harlem — that the Puerto Ricans
had "gone Communist." But the people of Marcantonio's
tenement domain neither knew nor cared what battles he
fought in Congress. Who in East Harlem has ever seen "Congress"? The battle his people knew and faced was the battle
with the landlord, and "Marc" was their hero and champion
in it.

Marcantonio got his political start in the old La Guardia
Club, and so did the Puerto Ricans — though in different
ways and for different reasons. Fiorello La Guardia first
spotted the talents of Marcantonio when he led a successful
tenants' strike at the age of twenty. Four years later, while he
was still a student at New York University Law School, he
managed La Guardia's successful campaign for a seat in the
U.S. Congress as Representative from East Harlem. That was
in 1924, and it was not until the early depression days of the
thirties that the Puerto Ricans began coming into the La
Guardia Club. They had taken no part in New York City
politics before that, and came on the scene through their own
necessity and the local politicians' growing awareness of their
potential voting strength in the area. One of the early Puerto
Rican members of the La Guardia Club recalls that many of
the Puerto Ricans first got involved "because of the depression."

"You had to go to your congressman to find out how to get
help. Well, they gave you the help and then wanted you to
help them back with your vote and political support. That's
how it started."

Puerto Rican participation was developed further by Marcantonio, who did not depend alone on his knowledge of Span-

ish to draw their support, but chose as his top lieutenant and "Spanish secretary" a bright young man from Arecibo, Puerto Rico, named Manuel Medina. Marcantonio had a special "secretary" at his club from each of the district's minority groups so that constituents of any shade of color or dialect could speak about their problems with a brother when they came to the club for help. At election time, Marcantonio would send these "secretaries" to campaign for him among their own particular minority; the dream of Willie Rodríguez in 1957 had already been realized twenty years before by Marcantonio, who had the right-language speaker for every section.

Marcantonio's Puerto Rican secretary, Manuel Medina, was a fiery speaker as well as an able administrator, and achieved considerable stature of his own in Spanish Harlem. He ran twice for office himself, in 1949 for state assembly, losing to the Negro Hulan Jack (who went on to become Borough President of Manhattan) by only 671 votes, and in 1950 made an impressive showing in the city council race by polling 27,853 votes and thereby coming closer than anyone since then to upsetting John J. Merli. Merli got 35,377 votes, which is the usual total the Democratic candidate roughly counts on in that district. In explaining his unexpected showing in the city council race, Medina made clear that he broke none of the neighborhood traditions in campaigning — he spoke only to the Puerto Ricans. As for the Italians, "Marc took care of that." But after Marcantonio was beaten by the coalition that same year, and died of a heart attack in August of 1954, after starting to talk again of a comeback, there has been no one to "take care of the Italians" — or even to talk to them — in behalf of a Puerto Rican candidate. Marcantonio's organization died with him, and Manuel Medina, one of Spanish Harlem's most well-known political figures, became a notary public at 100th and Madison.

It is true that no non–Puerto Rican politician in New York except Marcantonio captured the Puerto Ricans' support and sentiment, and it is also true that no politician except Marcantonio ever sincerely tried. The history of the city's politicians in their relations with the Puerto Ricans has been a history of flimsy "favors" of the most condescending kind. The "recognition" of the major political parties and their candidates of the Puerto Ricans in New York City has varied only in its degree of crudeness, and has always been limited to the most ingenious minimum of real help and a sickening maximum of grandiose "brotherhood" oratory.

The first recorded recognition of the Puerto Ricans by a major party's political candidate occurred when Senator Robert Wagner, Sr., made the magnanimous gesture of having lunch with a group of the leaders of the city's Puerto Rican community in 1932. The historic occasion was officially photographed and printed in the Spanish press of the city. Lunch was not to be scoffed at — it was more than the Puerto Ricans had received from any other politician, and represented the most liberal action yet carried out in their behalf.

The few scattered Puerto Rican political recognitions and victories since then have come through last-minute efforts of a party or candidate to play for the "Spanish vote." When the election was over, the people who cast the "Spanish vote" were again forgotten. The most flagrant use of this technique has come on the mayoralty level, where the candidates before election decide they must show their deep sensitivity to the problems of the Puerto Ricans. A handy and painless device for this was invented by Mayor William O'Dwyer six weeks before the 1949 elections for mayor in New York City. It is called "The Mayor's Committee on Puerto Rican Affairs." It passes manifestoes. It is referred to in the campaigns as evidence of the mayor's vital interest in the Spanish-speaking peoples of the city, who, potentially, make up the fourth largest "national" voting bloc, behind the Italians, Irish, and Jews. The Mayor's Committee on Puerto Rican Affairs, after proving its use as a harmless propaganda group, was solemnly adopted and incorporated by Mayor Vincent Impellitteri and then Mayor Robert Wagner, Jr. Recently, however, Wagner incorporated it into the Committee on Inter-Group Relations. It holds conferences and passes manifestoes. It has one Puerto Rican member.

In 1951 Mayor Vincent Impellitteri moved beyond the shadow play of his Committee on Puerto Rican Affairs to make a historic political appointment. He named Emilio Nuñez to the post of Special Sessions Justice, proudly proclaiming that this was the first Puerto Rican appointed to serve in the municipal court of New York. As it turned out, Emilio Nuñez did not happen to be a Puerto Rican. He had a Spanish name, of course — and, indeed, he was from Spain. In such ways the faceless minority confounds the politicians with the always surprising, always bothersome business of having some personal identity.

That was the last "Puerto Rican" political appointment until 1957. It was then that Mayor Wagner announced for the second time in New York City history the first appointment of a Puerto Rican to the post of municipal magistrate. The mayor made sure that his designee, Manuel Gómez, not only spoke Spanish, but also came from Puerto Rico. Manuel Gómez was the real thing and history was finally made.

The Puerto Ricans have fared only slightly better in getting into elective office. Two of them have made the New York State Assembly, and the first, surprisingly enough, was elected in the earliest days of Puerto Rican political participation. In 1937 the Republican Party was looking for a way to upset the Democrats in the old 17th (now the 14th) Assembly District in Spanish Harlem. It was composed of about half Negroes and half Puerto Ricans, and the Republicans hit on the novel notion of running a Puerto Rican. Oscar García Rivera was the man, and he won. The next year at Albany he voted for the type of legislation that would most benefit his tenement constituents and this did not happen to be the type of legislation being pushed by the Republican Party. García Rivera was accused by the Republican club of his district of "hanging around too much with Communists and members of the American Labor Party" and on these grounds was refused support for re-election and kicked out of the club. He turned to Marcantonio, and won a second term as a candidate of the American Labor Party before retiring from elective politics.

In 1953 Ed Flynn, boss of the Bronx Democratic Club, needed a candidate for state assembly and decided to make an appeal for the first time to the second oldest Puerto Rican community of the city, the Morrisania and Mott Haven section of the Bronx. A Puerto Rican named Felipe Torres was supported for state assembly by Flynn's club in 1953. He won then and still holds the seat.

The Democratic Party in Manhattan, party of the people, the masses, and minorities, managed to avoid ever running a Puerto Rican for any elected office until 1958 when it nominated and elected Jose Ramon Lopez to the state assembly from the East Harlem District. The Puerto Ricans who had previously run in their oldest neighborhood, in East

Harlem, had run on the tickets of the Republicans, the Liberals, and before it died, the American Labor Party. This is not necessarily a sign of the forward-looking nature of the aforementioned parties, but rather a tactic mixed of despair and hope by the out-of-office political groups to score an upset over the older, entrenched minorities represented by the ruling Democrats.

The first Democratic acknowledgment of Puerto Ricans in Spanish Harlem occurred in 1954 as a result of the fact that the Jewish District leader of the 14th A.D. had refused to support Robert Wagner, the Tammany Hall candidate for mayor, the previous year. The great majority of the Jewish community had long moved out of East Harlem — including Sammy Kantor, the Democratic district leader. But Sammy Kantor was entrenched, and might be to this day were it not for the fact that he threw his political cards with Vincent Impellitteri and thus aroused the wrath of DeSapio and Tammany Hall.

DeSapio "discovered" that Kantor did not actually live in his district any more and thereby had him disqualified from the local Democratic leadership. The fact that the leader did not live in his district was nothing strange. It is common practice for a political leader of a slum area, when he makes good as representative of his old neighborhood, to realize the dream of its residents and move to a better place.

Having ousted Kantor, DeSapio decided to recognize the people who were still unfortunate enough to live in the district, and appointed a Puerto Rican. He called before his throne a representative selection of Puerto Ricans and placed his hand on the shoulder of one named Antonio Méndez, a mild-mannered, hard-working gentleman who had a jewelry store in Spanish Harlem, no political past, and no recognizable ambitions of a political future beyond the one assigned him by DeSapio. The other candidates for the appointment included men who had worked as block captains in Sammy Kantor's club and had expressed certain hopes of someday running for an office. These more wild-eyed men were passed by. Tony Méndez thus became the first Puerto Rican district leader in New York City, and a new blow was struck for democracy. DeSapio further noted the bravery of his selection, since it was made at a time when much adverse publicity was going to the Puerto Ricans because of the shooting up of Congress by a group of Puerto Rican Nationalists. In appointing Méndez, DeSapio firmly stated that:

"The Democratic Party believes now, as it always did, that guilt by association is as tyrannic, as evil, and as ugly as Communism. The Democratic Party believes that the Puerto Rican people will provide leadership to our nation and add to our great heritage as a free people."

Thus having assured New York that Tony Méndez would lead no gunmen on City Hall, DeSapio seated him into the district leadership. He has done an earnest job, and has been faithful to the Chief through a growing number of bolts and threats to the status quo from within and without the club. The first official challenge to Tony's leadership occurred in the fall of 1957, when one of his top captains — a man who had hoped for the district leadership himself — opened a short-lived revolt. Benie Cabellero announced his candidacy for the leadership of the 14th A.D. East with a pink-and-blue leaflet charging that "Agitators, Pinkos, Nationalists, and Non-Residents Have Taken Over the Democratic Leadership of the 14th A.D. (East)."

To lead his attack against the cumulative evils noted on the leaflet, Benie had rented a headquarters and surrounded himself with dedicated partisans. There seemed to be a scarcity, however, of dedicated partisans. The long hall of Benie's headquarters, draped in the neighborhood tradition of loyalty with Puerto Rican and American flags, was far from being full on any given evening. Hoping to create a more convincing impression of strength, Benie had given a local mambo band the back of the hall to use for practice, and the music, noise, and bustle that they created gave the place a much more invigorating atmosphere. Some friends dropped by the hall one night to see how things were going, and Benie, a handsome, tall young man in slacks and an open-necked shirt with the sleeves rolled up (nose to the grindstone) got up from his desk that was barren except for the leaflets of his cause and, with a somewhat distracted air, began to size up the situation. This was particularly difficult because of the mambo band, which was going full steam ahead in the back of the hall. Benie gave several leaflets to the visitors, and one friend asked him how he could charge that poor Tony Méndez was both a Pinko and a Nationalist. Benie answered by saying that a much more basic issue was the one stated further on in the leaflet. He pointed to the following lines (quoted in the original spelling):

"We firmly believe that Tony Mendez, being illiterate and inixperienced in political matters, cannot lead the Puerto Rican people residents of this district effectively."

Benie elaborated on this by explaining in tones of outrage that Tony was very uneducated and Americans would think all Puerto Ricans were uneducated if Tony were the Puerto Rican district leader. "I'll tell you the truth," said Benie, "when Tony goes to see Carmine, he doesn't call him 'Chief' — he calls him 'Chef'!"

But Benie never got the chance to put his platform to the

test. The Chief had his men look into the revolt, and Benie's petitions to run against Tony were disqualified in court on grounds that they were not properly taken. Benie disappeared from the scene in disgrace, and was last reported to be living in Greenwich Village, which may mean something to the eventual literary, if not the political, history of the Puerto Ricans.

A much greater menace to the status quo of Tony's Caribe Club came shortly after when the Liberal Party announced that it was running José Lumen Román for the City Council in East Harlem. Tony's Puerto Rican Democratic Club would of course have to support the Italian Tammany incumbent, John J. Merli. Although he was given little chance of upsetting Merli, Román posed a solid and dangerous challenge to Tony Méndez's power, which would stand or fall on how well he would be able to hold the Puerto Ricans in the Democratic camp against a Puerto Rican candidate. The motto of the Tony Méndez Club is "I am a Democrat first and a Puerto Rican second," and now it was up to Tony to prove that his people followed the rule.

His club was bolted again, this time by a group of old-timers, some of whom had once aspired to his office, who said that they could not stay loyal now against a Puerto Rican candidate. They set up a rival club called the "Loyal Democrats" and reversed the motto of Tony's club for their own, saying "I am a Puerto Rican first, and a Democrat second."

This heresy was looked upon with horror by Tammany Hall, and in election week a group of regular Democratic candidates for city office spoke at a rally for the status quo at Tony's club, pounding home again the politics of acquiescence and obedience that constitutes their political message to the Puerto Ricans. The essence of this psychology is that everyone will be given his handout and it is unpatriotic to step out of line. The Italians are ahead of you, but they were there first. This Democratic ideal was summed up most cogently by one of Tammany's lawyers for the club, a man named Irwin Grey. He told the assembled Puerto Rican multitudes who crowded the club and stood drinking the beer and eating the bread that is the bounty of Tammany Hall for its people in election week rallies that:

"We must show that we will follow our leader to elect all Democrats running for office."

He explained that by doing this — by turning out a large vote in that mainly Puerto Rican district — it would endear the people to the Democratic leadership.

"And then, when we come here for little favors during the year, we will be strong and Tony will be able to ask the Mayor for many little favors for the Puerto Rican people."

The Democratic Party stands in the midst of the nation's worst slum and assures the people who live in its roach-ridden rooms that go for three times the price of a room south of 96th Street and are cursed by its landlords and robbed by its bosses and union leaders alike and have gone for the more than a hundred years that they have lived and worked in this city without a representative on its council that if they will turn out in force to vote for the Democratic Party they will be rewarded by little favors. Return us to power, says Irwin Grey, and we will serve you more beer and hot dogs when election time comes again, and your children out there who are put in "health classes" in the local grade schools because they suffer from malnutrition so badly they can't do their schoolwork, they can come too, and partake of the hot dogs that Carmine DeSapio dispenses as a favor.

Neither DeSapio nor Mayor Wagner appeared at the Democratic rally in Spanish Harlem. It was left to local candidates and third-string party hacks to deliver the high promise of a handout.

The Tony Méndez Club did its job, and proved its devotion to the cause beyond a doubt when it kicked out Frank Rodríguez, one of its workers who was caught on Election Day showing a Puerto Rican who came to ask how to vote for José Lumen Román how it was done. Political education has its limits.

Román's final appeal to the people came at an Election Eve rally at the Park Palace, a dance hall at 110th and Fifth Avenue. This is the northeast tip of Central Park, where the Irish squatters once had their huts, and now is lit by the red and blue neon sign of the Park Palace, and next to it, the dull blue neon cross of the Temple Bethel, Iglesia Evangélica Pentecostal. But despite the neon, the tip of the Park is a gloomy spot. It is here that the fine façade of apartments facing the Park on Fifth Avenue finally ends. On all the other avenues the slums of East Harlem begin at 96th Street, but Fifth keeps up its face of finery as far as 100th, although immediately behind it is the world of the tenements. But 110th and the end of the Park is also the end of Fifth Avenue's reach of extended comfort into Spanish Harlem. North of 110th the high, clean apartment buildings are replaced by the low, dingy tenement buildings, and the fine double-globed street lamps that line the Avenue also end and become instead the single lamps that stand, one to a block, in the upper, darker regions. Grouped at this crossroads the night before election was José Román and an assemblage of his faithful campaigners. Joe was wearing one of his campaign sombreros, and bearing an assortment of flowers and flags. About a half hour before the rally was to start he went with several aides in a waiting soundtruck to drive Pied Piper fashion through Spanish Harlem, luring the citizens on to the Palace.

But a little after the designated starting time, the inside of the Park Palace held something less than a hundred people. Joe Salvero of Local 485 of the International Union of Electrical Workers got the program going with a properly oratorical endorsement in behalf of Local 485 for Román, and in the midst of it Joe himself made his grand entrance. He was, however, followed by no great crowd of citizens. The audience rose, and Joe came down the center aisle, a Puerto Rican flag in one hand, an American flag in the other, and a woman behind him ringing a bell above his head as he walked. A few other friends followed behind. Joe took the platform and settled down to hear the long evening's speeches from representatives of 485, the Liberal Party, and Mrs. Cruz Torres, one of the defected leaders of the Caribe Club, who came to endorse Román and say, "I am here tonight not as a politician; I am here as a Puerto Rican." Nearly everyone made allusion to the historic nature of the occasion, and a Liberal Party speaker summed it up by predicting that "tomorrow will be a day of destiny."

But destiny was the same as it always was. A meager 5452 people pulled the C-line lever for Román, which is only slightly more than the usual total that any Liberal Party candidate expects in the 22nd Senatorial District. The Republican candidate, Richard Welden, got 10,460, which is the usual total a Republican runs up in the 22nd; largely through strong support in the "American" and "German" part of the district south of 96th Street. John Merli got 32,032, which was 3000 less than when he was first elected in 1950, but still quite close to the expected total that the Democrats count on in the area. The status quo was maintained to near perfection and Tony Méndez enforced his position as the faithful "House Puerto Rican" of Tammany Hall.

The results of the vote were almost identical with the party showings in the district in 1950 — except for the glaring absence of the 27,853 votes that Manuel Medina got on the American Labor Party line. Where did those 27,853 votes go? They were certainly largely Puerto Ricans. Medina himself feels that, for one thing, most of the Puerto Ricans who were registered and brought into politics by Marcantonio's organization merely gave up when "Marc" and his organization died; and that those who remained active went with the Democratic Party for lack of any alternative, and also, later on, because of the year-round work of Méndez and his club to line up the Puerto Ricans for the Democrats. If Román, as a Puerto Rican candidate, were to capitalize on the old power of Marcantonio's Puerto Rican following, and also bring out the new Puerto Rican residents, it would take time and money and men — none of which he had in any significant measure. He opened his headquarters two months before the election; two years would have hardly been enough. The registration of Puerto Ricans has always been difficult because of the literacy tests in English, which many are unable to take or embarrassed to try — especially in Spanish Harlem, which has an older age level than many of the newer Puerto Rican settlements, and is sufficient enough unto itself that people who live there (especially women, who don't have to go outside the area to look for jobs) are easily able to stay there all their lives without knowing a single word of English. Many do just that. The Council of Spanish Organizations in New York City estimated in 1957 that there were 85,000 Puerto Ricans registered to vote in the city of New York — and a potential total of 266,000 voters. The relatively small number who vote is not due to any "national" or "cultural" lack of interest in voting by Puerto Ricans, since elections in Puerto Rico usually draw 80 per cent of the voters. The difference in that and their percentage on the mainland can be attributed in some significant part to the language-test requirement. When the East Harlem Protestant Parish put on an extensive effort to register new residents for voting in 1956, they signed up hundreds of people who had lived in the neighborhood for years and had never voted. Many of the people still were reluctant to go and take the tests, and in many cases it was only the active persuasion of Ramón Diaz, talking, cajoling, pushing, encouraging, helping ladies on with coats and sticking hats on old men's heads to lead them to the polls, that got them signed up at all.

It is obvious that in any case the voting pattern in the Puerto Ricans' oldest neighborhood, the 22nd Senatorial District, was exactly the same in 1957 as it was in 1950, except for the lack of the ALP strength. And yet, there has been a tremendous new influx of residents since then, especially of Puerto Ricans into the formerly heavy Italian area east of Lexington Avenue, between 96th and 116th Streets. But that is largely the domain of John Merli's Democratic district assembly club, and it is against the continued survival of John Merli to go out and try to register the new Puerto Rican residents. There is no other organization to do it — Román in two months could hardly have begun.

Election night was only a postscript to all that had happened before in the campaign. But postscripts, though brief, are usually imperative, and often say something more essential than the text. I would like to tell you what election night was like in Spanish Harlem, for I think that by describing it I can best leave a postscript to all that has gone before in this book.

I set out to visit the headquarters of the candidates about nine o'clock that evening, but even by that early hour the candidates themselves had already left their followers to the respective isolations of victory and defeat. The isolated nature of the victory party at John Merli's headquarters on 105th Street was almost complete, for in the midst of that block of largely Puerto Rican residents there were only two Puerto Ricans in the crowd of celebrants. The rest of the gathering was made up of either Italians or cops. And the presence of the cops did nothing to change the "provincial" nature of the party, since their only stakes in the celebration were the roast beef sandwiches and beer of victory. I asked the nearest partisan when and if Mr. Merli would return, and he told me that the Councilman had gone home to see his aged mother in order to share the glad tidings with her. I nodded with respect and approval, but after my informant had moved away toward the beer, a slightly more shabby, bleary-eyed reveler who had overheard our conversation nudged me gently and said — the cigarette bobbing from the corner of his mouth as he spoke — that Merli had gone downtown to DeSapio's party for the Tammany victors and probably wouldn't be back at all. Thanking this honest Samaritan, I turned and left. Outside, the street was dark, and a slight drizzle of rain was falling. Campaign leaflets dropped by some last-minute toiler that day were scattered up and down the block, sticking to the wet sidewalk like the white, rectangular leaves of some artificial tree that was shedding its foliage in response to the close of an artificial season. I turned up the collar of my raincoat and walked west, toward Román's campaign headquarters.

At the corner of Third Avenue and 106th Street I stopped to look up at one of the rather bizarre posters that Robert Christenberry, the doomed Republican candidate for mayor, had put up throughout the city. The poster was an appeal to make New York "safe" again, and showed a young woman lying on the sidewalk, with several tough young boys in gang jackets standing above her. It might have been the cover for a dime thriller. I was about to walk on when I noticed that two teen-age boys were standing beside me, examining the poster. One of them turned to the other and speculated, "That must be those Juvenile Delinquents." The other boy nodded.

I walked straight on to Román's, only to find that Román himself had just left. There were no Italians, cops, nor refreshments to be found in the headquarters. The only citizens present besides the Puerto Ricans were a handful of volunteers from Local 485 of the International Union of Electrical Workers. That local has a growing Puerto Rican membership, and its leaders were interested in giving some support for the election of a Puerto Rican to the City Council. These outsiders from the local had worked every night with their Puerto Rican union brothers for the last two weeks of the election, and were known among Román's regulars as the only non-Spanish-speaking workers of the campaign. When I entered the headquarters, one of the Puerto Rican captains looked at me, smiled, and asked, "Are you Spanish?" I answered No, and he nodded understandingly, extended his hand, and said, "*Sholom Aleichem.*"

Several outsiders from the union who had stayed this late in the evening were finally saying goodbye, and I was the only "non-Spanish" visitor left. I went to the back of the hall where the few remaining workers stood around a desk among the scattered refuse of defeat — the useless maps and the leftover leaflets with the promise that "*los últimos serán los primeros*," the last shall be first; but the last were still last and the first were still first. The men passed around a pint of whiskey that someone had brought and talked in the bitterness of those who are always last. They talked of what was the mystery to them of their failure, blaming it finally on the Liberal Party, who they felt had not really cared, and pledging to form a Spanish party because they decided they could trust only themselves. I spoke up to ask if they didn't think this would limit their appeal to non-Spanish voters. There was silence for a moment as the men exchanged glances, and then one of them suddenly smiled and explained that it would be a "Spanish party open to all Americans." The others drank on that, but the happy effect of the momentary revelation was soon lost, and the group fell to silence again. After a while campaign manager Willie Rodríguez, his face pale and slightly whiskered by the long day, a notebook poking through a hole in his white shirt pocket, asked if he himself had failed, and the others assured him he had done his best. It was not his fault — it was the others, those forces that no one could quite pin down but which were against the Puerto Ricans; those invisible forces of bitterness and disregard which had again returned the Invisible Man to the City Council by an overwhelming vote, and the men around the desk stood beaten by them and not understanding them. Willie Rodríguez said there would be a meeting in that very room next Sunday to form the Spanish party. He stood for a moment in silence, then picked up the pint of whiskey, raised it in front of him, and proposed a toast.

"To the future," said Willie Rodríguez.